Michael E. Porter on Competition and Strategy

MICHAEL E. PORTER ON COMPETITION AND STRATEGY

A Harvard Business Review Paperback

Harvard Business Review paperback No. 90079

ISBN 0-87584-272-0

Contents

The Nature
of Competition

How competitive forces shape strategy

Awareness of these forces can help a company stake out a position in its industry that is less vulnerable to attack

Michael E. Porter

The nature and degree of competition in an industry hinge on five forces: the threat of new entrants, the bargaining power of customers, the bargaining power of suppliers, the threat of substitute products or services (where applicable), and the jockeying among current contestants.

To establish a strategic agenda for dealing with these contending currents and to grow despite them, a company must understand how they work in its industry and how they affect the company in its particular situation. The author details how these forces operate and suggests ways of adjusting to them, and, where possible, of taking advantage of them.

Mr. Porter is a specialist in industrial economics and business strategy. An associate professor of business administration at the Harvard Business School, he has created a course there entitled "Industry and Competitive Analysis." He sits on the boards of three companies and consults on strategy matters, and he has written many articles for economics journals and published two books. One of them, *Interbrand Choice, Strategy and Bilateral Market Power* (Harvard University Press, 1976) is an outgrowth of his doctoral thesis, for which he won the coveted Wells prize awarded by the Harvard economics department. He has recently completed two book manuscripts, one on competitive analysis in industry and the other (written with Michael Spence and Richard Caves) on competition in the open economy.

The essence of strategy formulation is coping with competition. Yet it is easy to view competition too narrowly and too pessimistically. While one sometimes hears executives complaining to the contrary, intense competition in an industry is neither coincidence nor bad luck.

Moreover, in the fight for market share, competition is not manifested only in the other players. Rather, competition in an industry is rooted in its underlying economics, and competitive forces exist that go well beyond the established combatants in a particular industry. Customers, suppliers, potential entrants, and substitute products are all competitors that may be more or less prominent or active depending on the industry.

The state of competition in an industry depends on five basic forces, which are diagrammed in the *Exhibit* on page 141. The collective strength of these forces determines the ultimate profit potential of an industry. It ranges from *intense* in industries like tires, metal cans, and steel, where no company earns spectacular returns on investment, to *mild* in industries like oil field services and equipment, soft drinks, and toiletries, where there is room for quite high returns.

In the economists' "perfectly competitive" industry, jockeying for position is unbridled and entry to the industry very easy. This kind of industry structure, of course, offers the worst prospect for long-run profitability. The weaker the forces collectively, however, the greater the opportunity for superior performance.

Whatever their collective strength, the corporate strategist's goal is to find a position in the industry where his or her company can best defend itself against these forces or can influence them in its favor. The collective strength of the forces may be painfully apparent to all the antagonists; but to cope with them, the strategist must delve below the surface and analyze the sources of each. For example, what makes the industry vulnerable to entry? What determines the bargaining power of suppliers?

Knowledge of these underlying sources of competitive pressure provides the groundwork for a strategic agenda of action. They highlight the critical strengths and weaknesses of the company, animate the positioning of the company in its industry, clarify the areas where strategic changes may yield the greatest payoff, and highlight the places where industry trends promise to hold the greatest significance as either opportunities or threats. Understanding these sources also proves to be of help in considering areas for diversification.

Contending forces

The strongest competitive force or forces determine the profitability of an industry and so are of greatest importance in strategy formulation. For example, even a company with a strong position in an industry unthreatened by potential entrants will earn low returns if it faces a superior or a lower-cost substitute product—as the leading manufacturers of vacuum tubes and coffee percolators have learned to their sorrow. In such a situation, coping with the substitute product becomes the number one strategic priority.

Different forces take on prominence, of course, in shaping competition in each industry. In the ocean-going tanker industry the key force is probably the buyers (the major oil companies), while in tires it is powerful OEM buyers coupled with tough competitors. In the steel industry the key forces are foreign competitors and substitute materials.

Every industry has an underlying structure, or a set of fundamental economic and technical characteristics, that gives rise to these competitive forces. The strategist, wanting to position his or her company to cope best with its industry environment or to influence that environment in the company's favor, must learn what makes the environment tick.

This view of competition pertains equally to industries dealing in services and to those selling products. To avoid monotony in this article, I refer to both products and services as "products." The same general principles apply to all types of business.

A few characteristics are critical to the strength of each competitive force. I shall discuss them in this section.

Threat of entry

New entrants to an industry bring new capacity, the desire to gain market share, and often substantial resources. Companies diversifying through acquisition into the industry from other markets often leverage their resources to cause a shake-up, as Philip Morris did with Miller beer.

The seriousness of the threat of entry depends on the barriers present and on the reaction from existing competitors that entrants can expect. If barriers to entry are high and newcomers can expect sharp retaliation from the entrenched competitors, obviously the newcomers will not pose a serious threat of entering.

There are six major sources of barriers to entry:

1. *Economies of scale*—These economies deter entry by forcing the aspirant either to come in on a large scale or to accept a cost disadvantage. Scale economies in production, research, marketing, and service are probably the key barriers to entry in the mainframe computer industry, as Xerox and GE sadly discovered. Economies of scale can also act as hurdles in distribution, utilization of the sales force, financing, and nearly any other part of a business.

2. *Product differentiation*—Brand identification creates a barrier by forcing entrants to spend heavily to overcome customer loyalty. Advertising, customer service, being first in the industry, and product differences are among the factors fostering brand identification. It is perhaps the most important entry barrier in soft drinks, over-the-counter drugs, cosmetics, investment banking, and public accounting. To create high fences around their businesses, brewers couple brand identification with economies of scale in production, distribution, and marketing.

3. *Capital requirements*—The need to invest large financial resources in order to compete creates a barrier to entry, particularly if the capital is required for unrecoverable expenditures in up-front advertising or R&D. Capital is necessary not only for fixed facilities but also for customer credit, inventories, and absorbing start-up losses. While major corporations have the financial resources to invade almost any industry, the huge capital requirements in certain fields, such as computer manufacturing and mineral extraction, limit the pool of likely entrants.

4. *Cost disadvantages independent of size*—Entrenched companies may have cost advantages not available to potential rivals, no matter what their

The experience curve as an entry barrier

In recent years, the experience curve has become widely discussed as a key element of industry structure. According to this concept, unit costs in many manufacturing industries (some dogmatic adherents say in *all* manufacturing industries) as well as in some service industries decline with "experience," or a particular company's cumulative volume of production. (The experience curve, which encompasses many factors, is a broader concept than the better-known learning curve, which refers to the efficiency achieved over a period of time by workers through much repetition.)

The causes of the decline in unit costs are a combination of elements, including economies of scale, the learning curve for labor, and capital-labor substitution. The cost decline creates a barrier to entry because new competitors with no "experience" face higher costs than established ones, particularly the producer with the largest market share, and have difficulty catching up with the entrenched competitors.

Adherents of the experience curve concept stress the importance of achieving market leadership to maximize this barrier to entry, and they recommend aggressive action to achieve it, such as price cutting in anticipation of falling costs in order to build volume. For the combatant that cannot achieve a healthy market share, the prescription is usually, "Get out."

Is the experience curve an entry barrier on which strategies should be built? The answer is: not in every industry. In fact, in some industries, building a strategy on the experience curve can be potentially disastrous. That costs decline with experience in some industries is not news to corporate executives. The significance of the experience curve for strategy depends on what factors are causing the decline.

If costs are falling because a growing company can reap economies of scale through more efficient, automated facilities and vertical integration, then the cumulative volume of production is unimportant to its relative cost position. Here the lowest-cost producer is the one with the largest, most efficient facilities.

A new entrant may well be more efficient than the more experienced competitors; if it has built the newest plant, it will face no disadvantage in having to catch up. The strategic prescription, "You must have the largest, most efficient plant," is a lot different from, "You must produce the greatest cumulative output of the item to get your costs down."

Whether a drop in costs with cumulative (not absolute) volume erects an entry barrier also depends on the sources of the decline. If costs go down because of technical advances known generally in the industry or because of the development of improved equipment that can be copied or purchased from equipment suppliers, the experience curve is no entry barrier at all—in fact, new or less experienced competitors may actually enjoy a cost *advantage* over the leaders. Free of the legacy of heavy past investments, the newcomer or less experienced competitor can purchase or copy the newest and lowest-cost equipment and technology.

If, however, experience can be kept proprietary, the leaders will maintain a cost advantage. But new entrants may require less experience to reduce their costs than the leaders needed. All this suggests that the experience curve can be a shaky entry barrier on which to build a strategy.

While space does not permit a complete treatment here, I want to mention a few other crucial elements in determining the appropriateness of a strategy built on the entry barrier provided by the experience curve:

☐ The height of the barrier depends on how important costs are to competition compared with other areas like marketing, selling, and innovation.

☐ The barrier can be nullified by product or process innovations leading to a substantially new technology and thereby creating an entirely new experience curve.* New entrants can leapfrog the industry leaders and alight on the new experience curve, to which those leaders may be poorly positioned to jump.

☐ If more than one strong company is building its strategy on the experience curve, the consequences can be nearly fatal. By the time only one rival is left pursuing such a strategy, industry growth may have stopped and the prospects of reaping the spoils of victory long since evaporated.

*For an example drawn from the history of the automobile industry, see William J. Abernathy and Kenneth Wayne, "The Limits of the Learning Curve," HBR September-October 1974, p.109.

---

size and attainable economies of scale. These advantages can stem from the effects of the learning curve (and of its first cousin, the experience curve), proprietary technology, access to the best raw materials sources, assets purchased at preinflation prices, government subsidies, or favorable locations. Sometimes cost advantages are legally enforceable, as they are through patents. (For an analysis of the much-discussed experience curve as a barrier to entry, see the ruled insert above.)

5. *Access to distribution channels*—The newcomer on the block must, of course, secure distribution of its product or service. A new food product, for example, must displace others from the supermarket shelf via price breaks, promotions, intense selling efforts, or some other means. The more limited the wholesale or retail channels are and the more that existing competitors have these tied up, obviously the tougher that entry into the industry will be. Sometimes this barrier is so high that, to surmount it, a new contestant must create its own distribution channels, as Timex did in the watch industry in the 1950s.

6. *Government policy*—The government can limit or even foreclose entry to industries with such controls as license requirements and limits on access to

raw materials. Regulated industries like trucking, liquor retailing, and freight forwarding are noticeable examples; more subtle government restrictions operate in fields like ski-area development and coal mining. The government also can play a major indirect role by affecting entry barriers through controls such as air and water pollution standards and safety regulations.

The potential rival's expectations about the reaction of existing competitors also will influence its decision on whether to enter. The company is likely to have second thoughts if incumbents have previously lashed out at new entrants or if:

☐ The incumbents possess substantial resources to fight back, including excess cash and unused borrowing power, productive capacity, or clout with distribution channels and customers.

☐ The incumbents seem likely to cut prices because of a desire to keep market shares or because of industrywide excess capacity.

☐ Industry growth is slow, affecting its ability to absorb the new arrival and probably causing the financial performance of all the parties involved to decline.

Changing conditions

From a strategic standpoint there are two important additional points to note about the threat of entry.

First, it changes, of course, as these conditions change. The expiration of Polaroid's basic patents on instant photography, for instance, greatly reduced its absolute cost entry barrier built by proprietary technology. It is not surprising that Kodak plunged into the market. Product differentiation in printing has all but disappeared. Conversely, in the auto industry economies of scale increased enormously with post-World War II automation and vertical integration—virtually stopping successful new entry.

Second, strategic decisions involving a large segment of an industry can have a major impact on the conditions determining the threat of entry. For example, the actions of many U.S. wine producers in the 1960s to step up product introductions, raise advertising levels, and expand distribution nationally surely strengthened the entry roadblocks by raising economies of scale and making access to distribution channels more difficult. Similarly, decisions by members of the recreational vehicle industry to vertically integrate in order to lower costs have greatly increased the economies of scale and raised the capital cost barriers.

Powerful suppliers & buyers

Suppliers can exert bargaining power on participants in an industry by raising prices or reducing the quality of purchased goods and services. Powerful suppliers can thereby squeeze profitability out of an industry unable to recover cost increases in its own prices. By raising their prices, soft drink concentrate producers have contributed to the erosion of profitability of bottling companies because the bottlers, facing intense competition from powdered mixes, fruit drinks, and other beverages, have limited freedom to raise *their* prices accordingly. Customers likewise can force down prices, demand higher quality or more service, and play competitors off against each other—all at the expense of industry profits.

The power of each important supplier or buyer group depends on a number of characteristics of its market situation and on the relative importance of its sales or purchases to the industry compared with its overall business.

A *supplier* group is powerful if:

☐ It is dominated by a few companies and is more concentrated than the industry it sells to.

☐ Its product is unique or at least differentiated, or if it has built up switching costs. Switching costs are fixed costs buyers face in changing suppliers. These arise because, among other things, a buyer's product specifications tie it to particular suppliers, it has invested heavily in specialized ancillary equipment or in learning how to operate a supplier's equipment (as in computer software), or its production lines are connected to the supplier's manufacturing facilities (as in some manufacture of beverage containers).

☐ It is not obliged to contend with other products for sale to the industry. For instance, the competition between the steel companies and the aluminum companies to sell to the can industry checks the power of each supplier.

☐ It poses a credible threat of integrating forward into the industry's business. This provides a check against the industry's ability to improve the terms on which it purchases.

☐ The industry is not an important customer of the supplier group. If the industry *is* an important customer, suppliers' fortunes will be closely tied to the industry, and they will want to protect the industry through reasonable pricing and assistance in activities like R&D and lobbying.

A *buyer* group is powerful if:

☐ It is concentrated or purchases in large volumes. Large-volume buyers are particularly potent forces if heavy fixed costs characterize the industry —as they do in metal containers, corn refining, and bulk chemicals, for example—which raise the stakes to keep capacity filled.

☐ The products it purchases from the industry are standard or undifferentiated. The buyers, sure that they can always find alternative suppliers, may play one company against another, as they do in aluminum extrusion.

☐ The products it purchases from the industry form a component of its product and represent a significant fraction of its cost. The buyers are likely to shop for a favorable price and purchase selectively. Where the product sold by the industry in question is a small fraction of buyers' costs, buyers are usually much less price sensitive.

☐ It earns low profits, which create great incentive to lower its purchasing costs. Highly profitable buyers, however, are generally less price sensitive (that is, of course, if the item does not represent a large fraction of their costs).

☐ The industry's product is unimportant to the quality of the buyers' products or services. Where the quality of the buyers' products is very much affected by the industry's product, buyers are generally less price sensitive. Industries in which this situation obtains include oil field equipment, where a malfunction can lead to large losses, and enclosures for electronic medical and test instruments, where the quality of the enclosure can influence the user's impression about the quality of the equipment inside.

☐ The industry's product does not save the buyer money. Where the industry's product or service can pay for itself many times over, the buyer is rarely price sensitive; rather, he is interested in quality. This is true in services like investment banking and public accounting, where errors in judgment can be costly and embarrassing, and in businesses like the logging of oil wells, where an accurate survey can save thousands of dollars in drilling costs.

☐ The buyers pose a credible threat of integrating backward to make the industry's product. The Big Three auto producers and major buyers of cars have often used the threat of self-manufacture as a bargaining lever. But sometimes an industry engenders a threat to buyers that its members may integrate forward.

Most of these sources of buyer power can be attributed to consumers as a group as well as to industrial and commercial buyers; only a modification of the frame of reference is necessary. Consumers tend to be more price sensitive if they are purchasing products that are undifferentiated, expen-

Exhibit
Forces governing competition in an industry

Threat of new entrants

Bargaining power of suppliers

The industry
Jockeying for position among current competitors

Bargaining power of customers

Threat of substitute products or services

sive relative to their incomes, and of a sort where quality is not particularly important.

The buying power of retailers is determined by the same rules, with one important addition. Retailers can gain significant bargaining power over manufacturers when they can influence consumers' purchasing decisions, as they do in audio components, jewelry, appliances, sporting goods, and other goods.

Strategic action

A company's choice of suppliers to buy from or buyer groups to sell to should be viewed as a crucial strategic decision. A company can improve its strategic posture by finding suppliers or buyers who possess the least power to influence it adversely.

Most common is the situation of a company being able to choose whom it will sell to—in other words, buyer selection. Rarely do all the buyer groups a company sells to enjoy equal power. Even if a company sells to a single industry, segments usually exist within that industry that exercise less power (and that are therefore less price sensitive) than others. For example, the replacement market for most products is less price sensitive than the overall market.

As a rule, a company can sell to powerful buyers and still come away with above-average profitability only if it is a low-cost producer in its industry or if its product enjoys some unusual, if not unique, features. In supplying large customers with electric motors, Emerson Electric earns high returns because its low cost position permits the company to meet or undercut competitors' prices.

If the company lacks a low cost position or a unique product, selling to everyone is self-defeating because the more sales it achieves, the more vulnerable it becomes. The company may have to muster the courage to turn away business and sell only to less potent customers.

Buyer selection has been a key to the success of National Can and Crown Cork & Seal. They focus on the segments of the can industry where they can create product differentiation, minimize the threat of backward integration, and otherwise mitigate the awesome power of their customers. Of course, some industries do not enjoy the luxury of selecting "good" buyers.

As the factors creating supplier and buyer power change with time or as a result of a company's strategic decisions, naturally the power of these groups rises or declines. In the ready-to-wear clothing industry, as the buyers (department stores and clothing stores) have become more concentrated and control has passed to large chains, the industry has come under increasing pressure and suffered falling margins. The industry has been unable to differentiate its product or engender switching costs that lock in its buyers enough to neutralize these trends.

Substitute products

By placing a ceiling on prices it can charge, substitute products or services limit the potential of an industry. Unless it can upgrade the quality of the product or differentiate it somehow (as via marketing), the industry will suffer in earnings and possibly in growth.

Manifestly, the more attractive the price-performance trade-off offered by substitute products, the firmer the lid placed on the industry's profit potential. Sugar producers confronted with the large-scale commercialization of high-fructose corn syrup, a sugar substitute, are learning this lesson today.

Substitutes not only limit profits in normal times; they also reduce the bonanza an industry can reap in boom times. In 1978 the producers of fiberglass insulation enjoyed unprecedented demand as a result of high energy costs and severe winter weather. But the industry's ability to raise prices was tempered by the plethora of insulation substitutes, including cellulose, rock wool, and styrofoam. These substitutes are bound to become an even stronger force once the current round of plant additions by fiberglass insulation producers has boosted capacity enough to meet demand (and then some).

Substitute products that deserve the most attention strategically are those that (a) are subject to trends improving their price-performance trade-off with the industry's product, or (b) are produced by industries earning high profits. Substitutes often come rapidly into play if some development increases competition in their industries and causes price reduction or performance improvement.

Jockeying for position

Rivalry among existing competitors takes the familiar form of jockeying for position—using tactics like price competition, product introduction, and advertising slugfests. Intense rivalry is related to the presence of a number of factors:

☐ Competitors are numerous or are roughly equal in size and power. In many U.S. industries in recent years foreign contenders, of course, have become part of the competitive picture.

☐ Industry growth is slow, precipitating fights for market share that involve expansion-minded members.

☐ The product or service lacks differentiation or switching costs, which lock in buyers and protect one combatant from raids on its customers by another.

☐ Fixed costs are high or the product is perishable, creating strong temptation to cut prices. Many basic materials businesses, like paper and aluminum, suffer from this problem when demand slackens.

☐ Capacity is normally augmented in large increments. Such additions, as in the chlorine and vinyl chloride businesses, disrupt the industry's supply-demand balance and often lead to periods of overcapacity and price cutting.

☐ Exit barriers are high. Exit barriers, like very specialized assets or management's loyalty to a particular business, keep companies competing even though they may be earning low or even negative returns on investment. Excess capacity remains functioning, and the profitability of the healthy competitors suffers as the sick ones hang on.[1] If the entire industry suffers from overcapacity, it may

1. For a more complete discussion of exit barriers and their implications for strategy, see my article, "Please Note Location of Nearest Exit," *California Management Review*, Winter 1976, p. 21.

seek government help—particularly if foreign competition is present.

☐ The rivals are diverse in strategies, origins, and "personalities." They have different ideas about how to compete and continually run head-on into each other in the process.

As an industry matures, its growth rate changes, resulting in declining profits and (often) a shakeout. In the booming recreational vehicle industry of the early 1970s, nearly every producer did well; but slow growth since then has eliminated the high returns, except for the strongest members, not to mention many of the weaker companies. The same profit story has been played out in industry after industry —snowmobiles, aerosol packaging, and sports equipment are just a few examples.

An acquisition can introduce a very different personality to an industry, as has been the case with Black & Decker's takeover of McCullough, the producer of chain saws. Technological innovation can boost the level of fixed costs in the production process, as it did in the shift from batch to continuous-line photo finishing in the 1960s.

While a company must live with many of these factors—because they are built into industry economics—it may have some latitude for improving matters through strategic shifts. For example, it may try to raise buyers' switching costs or increase product differentiation. A focus on selling efforts in the fastest-growing segments of the industry or on market areas with the lowest fixed costs can reduce the impact of industry rivalry. If it is feasible, a company can try to avoid confrontation with competitors having high exit barriers and can thus sidestep involvement in bitter price cutting.

Formulation of strategy

Once having assessed the forces affecting competition in an industry and their underlying causes, the corporate strategist can identify the company's strengths and weaknesses. The crucial strengths and weaknesses from a strategic standpoint are the company's posture vis-à-vis the underlying causes of each force. Where does it stand against substitutes? Against the sources of entry barriers?

Then the strategist can devise a plan of action that may include (1) positioning the company so that its capabilities provide the best defense against the competitive force; and/or (2) influencing the balance of the forces through strategic moves, thereby improving the company's position; and/or (3) anticipating shifts in the factors underlying the forces and responding to them, with the hope of exploiting change by choosing a strategy appropriate for the new competitive balance before opponents recognize it. I shall consider each strategic approach in turn.

Positioning the company

The first approach takes the structure of the industry as given and matches the company's strengths and weaknesses to it. Strategy can be viewed as building defenses against the competitive forces or as finding positions in the industry where the forces are weakest.

Knowledge of the company's capabilities and of the causes of the competitive forces will highlight the areas where the company should confront competition and where avoid it. If the company is a low-cost producer, it may choose to confront powerful buyers while it takes care to sell them only products not vulnerable to competition from substitutes.

The success of Dr Pepper in the soft drink industry illustrates the coupling of realistic knowledge of corporate strengths with sound industry analysis to yield a superior strategy. Coca-Cola and Pepsi-Cola dominate Dr Pepper's industry, where many small concentrate producers compete for a piece of the action. Dr Pepper chose a strategy of avoiding the largest-selling drink segment, maintaining a narrow flavor line, forgoing the development of a captive bottler network, and marketing heavily. The company positioned itself so as to be least vulnerable to its competitive forces while it exploited its small size.

In the $11.5 billion soft drink industry, barriers to entry in the form of brand identification, large-scale marketing, and access to a bottler network are enormous. Rather than accept the formidable costs and scale economies in having its own bottler network—that is, following the lead of the Big Two and of Seven-Up—Dr Pepper took advantage of the different flavor of its drink to "piggyback" on Coke and Pepsi bottlers who wanted a full line to sell to customers. Dr Pepper coped with the power of these buyers through extraordinary service and other efforts to distinguish its treatment of them from that of Coke and Pepsi.

Many small companies in the soft drink business offer cola drinks that thrust them into head-to-head competition against the majors. Dr Pepper, however, maximized product differentiation by maintaining a narrow line of beverages built around an unusual flavor.

Finally, Dr Pepper met Coke and Pepsi with an advertising onslaught emphasizing the alleged uniqueness of its single flavor. This campaign built strong brand identification and great customer loyalty. Helping its efforts was the fact that Dr Pepper's formula involved lower raw materials cost, which gave the company an absolute cost advantage over its major competitors.

There are no economies of scale in soft drink concentrate production, so Dr Pepper could prosper despite its small share of the business (6%). Thus Dr Pepper confronted competition in marketing but avoided it in product line and in distribution. This artful positioning combined with good implementation has led to an enviable record in earnings and in the stock market.

Influencing the balance

When dealing with the forces that drive industry competition, a company can devise a strategy that takes the offensive. This posture is designed to do more than merely cope with the forces themselves; it is meant to alter their causes.

Innovations in marketing can raise brand identification or otherwise differentiate the product. Capital investments in large-scale facilities or vertical integration affect entry barriers. The balance of forces is partly a result of external factors and partly in the company's control.

Exploiting industry change

Industry evolution is important strategically because evolution, of course, brings with it changes in the sources of competition I have identified. In the familiar product life-cycle pattern, for example, growth rates change, product differentiation is said to decline as the business becomes more mature, and the companies tend to integrate vertically.

These trends are not so important in themselves; what is critical is whether they affect the sources of competition. Consider vertical integration. In the maturing minicomputer industry, extensive vertical integration, both in manufacturing and in software development, is taking place. This very signif-

icant trend is greatly raising economies of scale as well as the amount of capital necessary to compete in the industry. This in turn is raising barriers to entry and may drive some smaller competitors out of the industry once growth levels off.

Obviously, the trends carrying the highest priority from a strategic standpoint are those that affect the most important sources of competition in the industry and those that elevate new causes to the forefront. In contract aerosol packaging, for example, the trend toward less product differentiation is now dominant. It has increased buyers' power, lowered the barriers to entry, and intensified competition.

The framework for analyzing competition that I have described can also be used to predict the eventual profitability of an industry. In long-range planning the task is to examine each competitive force, forecast the magnitude of each underlying cause, and then construct a composite picture of the likely profit potential of the industry.

The outcome of such an exercise may differ a great deal from the existing industry structure. Today, for example, the solar heating business is populated by dozens and perhaps hundreds of companies, none with a major market position. Entry is easy, and competitors are battling to establish solar heating as a superior substitute for conventional methods.

The potential of this industry will depend largely on the shape of future barriers to entry, the improvement of the industry's position relative to substitutes, the ultimate intensity of competition, and the power captured by buyers and suppliers. These characteristics will in turn be influenced by such factors as the establishment of brand identities, significant economies of scale or experience curves in equipment manufacture wrought by technological change, the ultimate capital costs to compete, and the extent of overhead in production facilities.

The framework for analyzing industry competition has direct benefits in setting diversification strategy. It provides a road map for answering the extremely difficult question inherent in diversification decisions: "What is the potential of this business?" Combining the framework with judgment in its application, a company may be able to spot an industry with a good future before this good future is reflected in the prices of acquisition candidates.

2. Theodore Levitt, "Marketing Myopia," reprinted as an HBR Classic, September–October 1975, p. 26.

Multifaceted rivalry

Corporate managers have directed a great deal of attention to defining their businesses as a crucial step in strategy formulation. Theodore Levitt, in his classic 1960 article in HBR, argued strongly for avoiding the myopia of narrow, product-oriented industry definition.[2] Numerous other authorities have also stressed the need to look beyond product to function in defining a business, beyond national boundaries to potential international competition, and beyond the ranks of one's competitors today to those that may become competitors tomorrow. As a result of these urgings, the proper definition of a company's industry or industries has become an endlessly debated subject.

One motive behind this debate is the desire to exploit new markets. Another, perhaps more important motive is the fear of overlooking latent sources of competition that someday may threaten the industry. Many managers concentrate so single-mindedly on their direct antagonists in the fight for market share that they fail to realize that they are also competing with their customers and their suppliers for bargaining power. Meanwhile, they also neglect to keep a wary eye out for new entrants to the contest or fail to recognize the subtle threat of substitute products.

The key to growth—even survival—is to stake out a position that is less vulnerable to attack from head-to-head opponents, whether established or new, and less vulnerable to erosion from the direction of buyers, suppliers, and substitute goods. Establishing such a position can take many forms—solidifying relationships with favorable customers, differentiating the product either substantively or psychologically through marketing, integrating forward or backward, establishing technological leadership.▽

Reprint 79208

Corporate
Competitive Advantage

From competitive advantage to corporate strategy

Michael E. Porter

Corporate strategy, the overall plan for a diversified company, is both the darling and the stepchild of contemporary management practice – the darling because CEOs have been obsessed with diversification since the early 1960s, the stepchild because almost no consensus exists about what corporate strategy is, much less about how a company should formulate it.

The track record of corporate strategies has been dismal.

A diversified company has two levels of strategy: business unit (or competitive) strategy and corporate (or companywide) strategy. Competitive strategy concerns how to create competitive advantage in each of the businesses in which a company competes. Corporate strategy concerns two different questions: what businesses the corporation should be in and how the corporate office should manage the array of business units.

Corporate strategy is what makes the corporate whole add up to more than the sum of its business unit parts.

The track record of corporate strategies has been dismal. I studied the diversification records of 33 large, prestigious U.S. companies over the 1950-1986 period and found that most of them had divested many more acquisitions than they had kept.

The corporate strategies of most companies have dissipated instead of created shareholder value.

The need to rethink corporate strategy could hardly be more urgent. By taking over companies and breaking them up, corporate raiders thrive on failed corporate strategy. Fueled by junk bond financing and growing acceptability, raiders can expose any company to takeover, no matter how large or blue chip.

Recognizing past diversification mistakes, some companies have initiated large-scale restructuring programs. Others have done nothing at all. Whatever the response, the strategic questions persist. Those who have restructured must decide what to do next to avoid repeating the past; those who have done nothing must awake to their vulnerability. To survive, companies must understand what good corporate strategy is.

A sober picture

While there is disquiet about the success of corporate strategies, none of the available evidence satisfactorily indicates the success or failure of corporate strategy. Most studies have approached the question by measuring the stock market valuation of

Michael E. Porter is professor of business administration at the Harvard Business School and author of Competitive Advantage *(Free Press, 1985) and* Competitive Strategy *(Free Press, 1980).*

Exhibit I	**Diversification profiles of 33 leading U.S. companies**

Company	Number total entries	All entries into new industries	Percent acqui- sitions	Percent joint ventures	Percent start-ups
ALCO Standard	221	165	99 %	0 %	1 %
Allied Corp.	77	49	67	10	22
Beatrice	382	204	97	1	2
Borden	170	96	77	4	19
CBS	148	81	67	16	17
Continental Group	75	47	77	6	17
Cummins Engine	30	24	54	17	29
Du Pont	80	39	33	16	51
Exxon	79	56	34	5	61
General Electric	160	108	47	20	33
General Foods	92	53	91	4	6
General Mills	110	102	84	7	9
W.R.Grace	275	202	83	7	10
Gulf & Western	178	140	91	4	6
IBM	46	38	18	18	63
IC Industries	67	41	85	3	12
ITT	246	178	89	2	9
Johnson & Johnson	88	77	77	0	23
Mobil	41	32	53	16	31
Procter & Gamble	28	23	61	0	39
Raytheon	70	58	86	9	5
RCA	53	46	35	15	50
Rockwell	101	75	73	24	3
Sara Lee	197	141	96	1	4
Scovill	52	36	97	0	3
Signal	53	45	67	4	29
Tenneco	85	62	81	6	13
3M	144	125	54	2	45
TRW	119	82	77	10	13
United Technologies	62	49	57	18	24
Westinghouse	129	73	63	11	26
Wickes	71	47	83	0	17
Xerox	59	50	66	6	28
Total	**3,788**	**2,644**			
Average	**114.8**	**80.1**	**70.3 %**	**7.9 %**	**21.8 %**

Note:
Beatrice, Continental Group, General Foods, RCA, Scovill, and Signal were taken over as the study was being completed. Their data cover the period up through takeover but not subsequent divestments.

Entries into new industries that represented entirely new fields	Percent acquisitions	Percent joint ventures	Percent start-ups
56	100 %	0 %	0 %
17	65	6	29
61	97	0	3
32	75	3	22
28	65	21	14
19	79	11	11
13	46	23	31
19	37	0	63
17	29	6	65
29	48	14	38
22	86	5	9
27	74	7	19
66	74	5	21
48	88	2	10
16	19	0	81
17	88	6	6
50	92	0	8
18	56	0	44
15	60	7	33
14	79	0	21
16	81	19	6
19	37	21	42
27	74	22	4
41	95	2	2
12	92	0	8
20	75	0	25
26	73	8	19
34	71	3	56
28	64	11	25
17	23	17	39
36	61	3	36
22	68	0	32
18	50	11	39
906			
27.4	**67.9 %**	**7.0 %**	**25.9 %**

Note:
The percentage averages may not add up
to 100% because of rounding off.

mergers, captured in the movement of the stock prices of acquiring companies immediately before and after mergers are announced.

These studies show that the market values mergers as neutral or slightly negative, hardly cause for serious concern.[1] Yet the short-term market reaction is a highly imperfect measure of the long-term success of diversification, and no self-respecting executive would judge a corporate strategy this way.

Studying the diversification programs of a company over a long period of time is a much more telling way to determine whether a corporate strategy has succeeded or failed. My study of 33 companies, many of which have reputations for good management, is a unique look at the track record of major corporations. (For an explanation of the research, see the insert "Where the Data Come From.") Each company entered an average of 80 new industries and 27 new fields. Just over 70% of the new entries were acquisitions, 22% were start-ups, and 8% were joint ventures. IBM, Exxon, Du Pont, and 3M, for example, focused on start-ups, while ALCO Standard, Beatrice, and Sara Lee diversified almost solely through acquisitions (Exhibit I has a complete rundown).

My data paint a sobering picture of the success ratio of these moves (see Exhibit II). I found that on average corporations divested more than half their acquisitions in new industries and more than 60% of their acquisitions in entirely new fields. Fourteen companies left more than 70% of all the acquisitions they had made in new fields. The track record in unrelated acquisitions is even worse – the average divestment rate is a startling 74% (see Exhibit III). Even a highly respected company like General Electric divested a very high percentage of its acquisitions, particularly those in new fields. Companies near the top of the list in Exhibit II achieved a remarkably low rate of divestment. Some bear witness to the success of well-thought-out corporate strategies. Others, however, enjoy a lower rate simply because they have not faced up to their problem units and divested them.

I calculated total shareholder returns (stock price appreciation plus dividends) over the period of the study for each company so that I could compare them with its divestment rate. While companies near the top of the list have above-average shareholder returns, returns are not a reliable measure of diversification success. Shareholder return often depends heavily on the inherent attractiveness of companies' base industries. Companies like CBS and General Mills had extremely profitable base businesses that subsidized poor diversification track records.

I would like to make one comment on the use of shareholder value to judge performance. Linking shareholder value quantitatively to diversification performance only works if you compare the shareholder value that is with the shareholder value that might have been without diversification. Because such a comparison is virtually impossible to make, my own measure of diversification success – the number of units retained by the company – seems to be as good an indicator as any of the contribution of diversification to corporate performance.

My data give a stark indication of the failure of corporate strategies.[2] Of the 33 companies, 6 had been taken over as my study was being completed (see the note on *Exhibit II*). Only the lawyers, investment bankers, and original sellers have prospered in most of these acquisitions, not the shareholders.

Premises of corporate strategy

Any successful corporate strategy builds on a number of premises. These are facts of life about diversification. They cannot be altered, and when ignored, they explain in part why so many corporate strategies fail.

Competition occurs at the business unit level. Diversified companies do not compete; only their business units do. Unless a corporate strategy places primary attention on nurturing the success of each unit, the strategy will fail, no matter how elegantly constructed. Successful corporate strategy must grow out of and reinforce competitive strategy.

Diversification inevitably adds costs and constraints to business units. Obvious costs such as the corporate overhead allocated to a unit may not be as important or subtle as the hidden costs and constraints. A business unit must explain its decisions to top management, spend time complying with planning and other corporate systems, live with parent company guidelines and personnel policies, and forgo the opportunity to motivate employees with direct equity ownership. These costs and constraints can be reduced but not entirely eliminated.

Shareholders can readily diversify themselves. Shareholders can diversify their own portfolios of stocks by selecting those that best match their preferences and risk profiles.[3] Shareholders can often diversify more cheaply than a corporation because they can buy shares at the market price and avoid hefty acquisition premiums.

These premises mean that corporate strategy cannot succeed unless it truly adds value – to business units by providing tangible benefits that offset the inherent costs of lost independence and to

shareholders by diversifying in a way they could not replicate.

Passing the essential tests

To understand how to formulate corporate strategy, it is necessary to specify the conditions under which diversification will truly create shareholder value. These conditions can be summarized in three essential tests:

1 **The attractiveness test.** The industries chosen for diversification must be structurally attractive or capable of being made attractive.

2 **The cost-of-entry test.** The cost of entry must not capitalize all the future profits.

3 **The better-off test.** Either the new unit must gain competitive advantage from its link with the corporation or vice versa.

Of course, most companies will make certain that their proposed strategies pass some of these tests. But my study clearly shows that when companies ignored one or two of them, the strategic results were disastrous.

How attractive is the industry?

In the long run, the rate of return available from competing in an industry is a function of its underlying structure, which I have described in another HBR article.[4] An attractive industry with a high average return on investment will be difficult to enter because entry barriers are high, suppliers and buyers have only modest bargaining power, substitute products or services are few, and the rivalry among competitors is stable. An unattractive industry like steel will have structural flaws, including a plethora of substitute materials, powerful and price-sensitive buyers, and excessive rivalry caused by high fixed costs and a large group of competitors, many of whom are state supported.

Diversification cannot create shareholder value unless new industries have favorable structures that support returns exceeding the cost of capital. If the industry doesn't have such returns, the company must be able to restructure the industry or gain a sustainable competitive advantage that leads to returns well above the industry average. An industry need not be attractive before diversification. In fact, a

Where the data come from

We studied the 1950-1986 diversification histories of 33 large diversified U.S. companies. They were chosen at random from many broad sectors of the economy.

To eliminate distortions caused by World War II, we chose 1950 as the base year and then identified each business the company was in. We tracked every acquisition, joint venture, and start-up made over this period – 3,788 in all. We classified each as an entry into an entirely new sector or field (financial services, for example), a new industry within a field the company was already in (insurance, for example), or a geographic extension of an existing product or service. We also classified each new field as related or unrelated to existing units. Then we tracked whether and when each entry was divested or shut down and the number of years each remained part of the corporation.

Our sources included annual reports, 10K forms, the F&S Index, and Moody's, supplemented by our judgment and general knowledge of the industries involved. In a few cases, we asked the companies specific questions.

It is difficult to determine the success of an entry without knowing the full purchase or start-up price, the profit history, the amount and timing of ongoing investments made in the unit, whether any write-offs or write-downs were taken, and the selling price and terms of sale. Instead, we employed a relatively simple way to gauge success: *whether the entry was divested or shut down.* The underlying assumption is that a company will gen-

erally not divest or close down a successful business except in a comparatively few special cases. Companies divested many of the entries in our sample within five years, a reflection of disappointment with performance. Of the comparatively few divestments where the company disclosed a loss or a gain, the divestment resulted in a reported loss in more than half the cases.

The data in *Exhibit I* cover the entire 1950-1986 period. However, the divestment ratios in *Exhibit II* and *Exhibit III* do not compare entries and divestments over the entire period because doing so would overstate the success of diversification. Companies usually do not shut down or divest new entries immediately but hold them for some time to give them an opportunity to succeed. Our data show that the average holding period is five to slightly more than ten years, though many divestments occur within five years. To accurately gauge the success of diversification, we calculated the percentage of entries made by 1975 and by 1980 that were divested or closed down as of January 1987. If we had included more recent entries, we would have biased upward our assessment of how successful these entries had been.

As compiled, these data probably understate the rate of failure. Companies tend to announce acquisitions and other forms of new entry with a flourish but divestments and shutdowns with a whimper, if at all. We have done our best to root out every such transaction, but we have undoubtedly missed some. There may also be new entries that we did not uncover, but our best impression is that the number is not large.

---

company might benefit from entering before the industry shows its full potential. The diversification can then transform the industry's structure.

In my research, I often found companies had suspended the attractiveness test because they had a vague belief that the industry "fit" very closely with their own businesses. In the hope that the corporate "comfort" they felt would lead to a happy outcome, the companies ignored fundamentally poor industry structures. Unless the close fit allows substantial competitive advantage, however, such comfort will turn into pain when diversification results in poor returns. Royal Dutch Shell and other leading oil companies have had this unhappy experience in a number of chemicals businesses, where poor industry structures overcame the benefits of vertical integration and skills in process technology.

Another common reason for ignoring the attractiveness test is a low entry cost. Sometimes the buyer has an inside track or the owner is anxious to sell. Even if the price is actually low, however, a one-

shot gain will not offset a perpetually poor business. Almost always, the company finds it must reinvest in the newly acquired unit, if only to replace fixed assets and fund working capital.

Diversifying companies are also prone to use rapid growth or other simple indicators as a proxy for a target industry's attractiveness. Many that rushed into fast-growing industries (personal computers, video games, and robotics, for example) were burned because they mistook early growth for long-term profit potential. Industries are profitable not because they are sexy or high tech; they are profitable only if their structures are attractive.

What is the cost of entry?

Diversification cannot build shareholder value if the cost of entry into a new business eats up its expected returns. Strong market forces,

| Exhibit II | **Acquisition track records of leading U.S. diversifiers ranked by percent divested** |

Company	All acquisitions in new industries	Percent made by 1980 and then divested	Percent made by 1975 and then divested	Acquisitions in new industries that represented entirely new fields	Percent made by 1980 and then divested	Percent made by 1975 and then divested
Johnson & Johnson	59	17 %	12 %	10	33 %	14 %
Procter & Gamble	14	17	17	11	17	17
Raytheon	50	17	26	13	25	33
United Technologies	28	25	13	10	17	0
3M	67	26	27	24	42	45
TRW	63	27	31	18	40	38
IBM	7	33	0*	3	33	0*
Du Pont	13	38	43	7	60	75
Mobil	17	38	57	9	50	50
Borden	74	39	40	24	45	50
IC Industries	35	42	50	15	46	44
Tenneco	50	43	47	19	27	33
Beatrice	198	46	45	59	52	51
ITT	159	52	52	46	61	61
Rockwell	55	56	57	20	71	71
Allied Corp.	33	57	45	11	80	67
Exxon	19	62	20*	5	80	50*
Sara Lee	135	62	65	39	80	76
General Foods	48	63	62	19	93	93
Scovill	35	64	77	11	64	70
Signal	30	65	63	15	70	67
ALCO Standard	164	65	70	56	72	76
W.R. Grace	167	65	70	49	71	70
General Electric	51	65	78	14	100	100
Wickes	38	67	72	15	73	70
Westinghouse	46	68	69	22	61	59
Xerox	33	71	79	9	100	100
Continental Group	36	71	72	15	60	60
General Mills	86	75	73	20	65	60
Gulf & Western	127	79	78	42	75	72
Cummins Engine	13	80	80	6	83	83
RCA	16	80	92	7	86	100
CBS	54	87	89	18	88	88
Total	**2,021**			**661**		
Average per company†	**61.2**	**53.4 %**	**56.5 %**	**20.0**	**61.2 %**	**61.1 %**

*Companies with three or fewer acquisitions by the cutoff year.

†Companies with three or fewer acquisitions by the cutoff year are excluded from the average to minimize statistical distortions.

Note:
Beatrice, Continental Group, General Foods, RCA, Scovill, and Signal were taken over as the study was being completed. Their data cover the period up through takeover but not subsequent divestments.

however, are working to do just that. A company can enter new industries by acquisition or start-up. Acquisitions expose it to an increasingly efficient merger market. An acquirer beats the market if it pays a price not fully reflecting the prospects of the new unit. Yet multiple bidders are commonplace, information flows rapidly, and investment bankers and other intermediaries work aggressively to make the market as efficient as possible. In recent years, new financial instruments such as junk bonds have brought new buyers into the market and made even large companies vulnerable to takeover. Acquisition premiums are high and reflect the acquired company's future prospects — sometimes too well. Philip Morris paid more than four times book value for Seven-Up Company, for example. Simple arithmetic meant that profits had to more than quadruple to sustain the preacquisition ROI. Since there proved to be little Philip Morris could add in marketing prowess to the sophisticated marketing wars in the soft-drink industry, the result was the unsatisfactory financial performance of Seven-Up and ultimately the decision to divest.

In a start-up, the company must overcome entry barriers. It's a real catch-22 situation, however, since attractive industries are attractive because their entry barriers are high. Bearing the full cost of the entry barriers might well dissipate any potential profits. Otherwise, other entrants to the industry would have already eroded its profitability.

In the excitement of finding an appealing new business, companies sometimes forget to apply the cost-of-entry test. The more attractive a new industry, the more expensive it is to get into.

Will the business be better off?

A corporation must bring some significant competitive advantage to the new unit, or the new unit must offer potential for significant advantage to the corporation. Sometimes, the benefits to the new unit accrue only once, near the time of entry, when the parent instigates a major overhaul of its strategy or installs a first-rate management team. Other diversification yields ongoing competitive advantage if the new unit can market its product through the well-developed distribution system of its sister units, for instance. This is one of the important underpinnings of the merger of Baxter Travenol and American Hospital Supply.

When the benefit to the new unit comes only once, the parent company has no rationale for holding the new unit in its portfolio over the long term. Once the results of the one-time improvement are clear, the diversified company no longer adds value to offset the inevitable costs imposed on the unit. It is best to sell the unit and free up corporate resources.

The better-off test does not imply that diversifying corporate risk creates shareholder value in and of itself. Doing something for shareholders that they can do themselves is not a basis for corporate strategy. (Only in the case of a privately held company, in which the company's and the shareholder's risk are the same, is diversification to reduce risk valuable for its own sake.) Diversification of risk should only be a by-product of corporate strategy, not a prime motivator.

Executives ignore the better-off test most of all or deal with it through arm waving or trumped-up logic rather than hard strategic analysis. One reason is that they confuse company size with shareholder value. In the drive to run a bigger company, they lose sight of their real job. They may justify the suspension of the better-off test by pointing to the way they manage diversity. By cutting corporate staff to the bone and giving business units nearly complete autonomy, they believe they avoid the pitfalls. Such thinking misses the whole point of diversification, which is to create shareholder value rather than to avoid destroying it.

Concepts of corporate strategy

The three tests for successful diversification set the standards that any corporate strategy must meet; meeting them is so difficult that most diversification fails. Many companies lack a clear concept of corporate strategy to guide their diversification or pursue a concept that does not address the tests. Others fail because they implement a strategy poorly.

My study has helped me identify four concepts of corporate strategy that have been put into practice — portfolio management, restructuring, transferring skills, and sharing activities. While the concepts are not always mutually exclusive, each rests on a different mechanism by which the corporation creates shareholder value and each requires the diversified company to manage and organize itself in a different way. The first two require no connections among business units; the second two depend on them. (See *Exhibit IV*.) While all four concepts of strategy have succeeded under the right circumstances, today some make more sense than others. Ignoring any of the concepts is perhaps the quickest road to failure.

Portfolio management

The concept of corporate strategy most in use is portfolio management, which is based primar-

Exhibit III	**Diversification performance in joint ventures, start-ups, and unrelated acquisitions**
	Companies in same order as in Exhibit II

Company	Joint ventures as a percent of new entries	Percent made by 1980 and then divested	Percent made by 1975 and then divested	Start-ups as a percent of new entries	Percent made by 1980 and then divested
Johnson & Johnson	0 %	†	†	23 %	14 %
Procter & Gamble	0	†	†	39	0
Raytheon	9	60 %	60 %	5	50
United Technologies	18	50	50	24	11
3M	2	100*	100*	45	2
TRW	10	20	25	13	63
IBM	18	100*	†	63	20
Du Pont	16	100*	†	51	61
Mobil	16	33	33	31	50
Borden	4	33	33	19	17
IC Industries	3	100*	100*	13	80
Tenneco	6	67	67	13	67
Beatrice	1	†	†	2	0
ITT	2	0*	†	8	38
Rockwell	24	38	42	3	0
Allied Corp.	10	100	75	22	38
Exxon	5	0	0	61	27
Sara Lee	1	†	†	4	75
General Foods	4	†	†	6	67
Scovill	0	†	†	3	100
Signal	4	†	†	29	20
ALCO Standard	0	†	†	1	†
W.R. Grace	7	33	38	10	71
General Electric	20	20	33	33	33
Wickes	0	†	†	17	63
Westinghouse	11	0*	0*	26	44
Xerox	6	100*	100*	28	50
Continental Group	6	67	67	17	14
General Mills	7	71	71	9	89
Gulf & Western	4	75	50	6	100
Cummins Engine	17	50	50	29	0
RCA	15	67	67	50	99
CBS	16	71	71	17	86
Average per company‡	**7.9 %**	**50.3 %**	**48.9 %**	**21.8 %**	**44.0 %**

*Companies with two or fewer entries.

†No entries in this category.

‡Average excludes companies with two or fewer entries to minimize statistical distortions.

Note:
Beatrice, Continental Group, General Foods, RCA, Scovill, and Signal were taken over as the study was being completed. Their data cover the period up through takeover but not subsequent divestments.

Percent made by 1975 and then divested	Acquisitions in unrelated new fields as a percent of total acquisitions in new fields	Percent made by 1980 and then divested	Percent made by 1975 and then divested
20 %	0 %	†	†
0	9	†	†
50	46	40 %	40 %
20	40	0*	0*
3	33	75	86
71	39	71	71
22	33	100*	100*
61	43	0*	0*
56	67	60	100
13	21	80	80
30	33	50	50
80	42	33	40
0	63	59	53
57	61	67	64
0	35	100	100
29	45	50	0
19	100	80	50*
100*	41	73	73
50	42	86	83
100*	45	80	100
11	67	50	50
†	63	79	81
71	39	65	65
44	36	100	100
57	60	80	75
44	36	57	67
56	22	100	100
0	40	83	100
80	65	77	67
100	74	77	74
0	67	100	100
55	36	100	100
80	39	100	100
40.9 %	**46.1 %**	**74.0 %**	**74.4 %**

ily on diversification through acquisition. The corporation acquires sound, attractive companies with competent managers who agree to stay on. While acquired units do not have to be in the same industries as existing units, the best portfolio managers generally limit their range of businesses in some way, in part to limit the specific expertise needed by top management.

The acquired units are autonomous, and the teams that run them are compensated according to unit results. The corporation supplies capital and works with each to infuse it with professional management techniques. At the same time, top management provides objective and dispassionate review of business unit results. Portfolio managers categorize units by potential and regularly transfer resources from units that generate cash to those with high potential and cash needs.

In a portfolio strategy, the corporation seeks to create shareholder value in a number of ways. It uses its expertise and analytical resources to spot attractive acquisition candidates that the individual shareholder could not. The company provides capital on favorable terms that reflect corporatewide fundraising ability. It introduces professional management skills and discipline. Finally, it provides high-quality review and coaching, unencumbered by conventional wisdom or emotional attachments to the business.

The logic of the portfolio management concept rests on a number of vital assumptions. If a company's diversification plan is to meet the attractiveness and cost-of-entry tests, it must find good but undervalued companies. Acquired companies must be truly undervalued because the parent does little for the new unit once it is acquired. To meet the better-off test, the benefits the corporation provides must yield a significant competitive advantage to acquired units. The style of operating through highly autonomous business units must both develop sound business strategies and motivate managers.

In most countries, the days when portfolio management was a valid concept of corporate strategy are past. In the face of increasingly well-developed capital markets, attractive companies with good managements show up on everyone's computer screen and attract top dollar in terms of acquisition premium. Simply contributing capital isn't contributing much. A sound strategy can easily be funded; small to medium-size companies don't need a munificent parent.

Other benefits have also eroded. Large companies no longer corner the market for professional management skills; in fact, more and more observers believe managers cannot necessarily run anything in the absence of industry-specific knowledge and experience. Another supposed advantage of the portfolio management concept—dispassionate review—rests on similarly shaky ground since the added value of review alone is questionable in a portfolio of sound companies.

The benefit of giving business units complete autonomy is also questionable. Increasingly, a company's business units are interrelated, drawn together by new technology, broadening distribution channels, and changing regulations. Setting strategies of units independently may well undermine unit performance. The companies in my sample that have succeeded in diversification have recognized the value of interrelationships and understood that a strong sense of corporate identity is as important as slavish adherence to parochial business unit financial results.

But it is the sheer complexity of the management task that has ultimately defeated even the best portfolio managers. As the size of the company grows, portfolio managers need to find more and more deals just to maintain growth. Supervising dozens or even hundreds of disparate units and under chain-letter pressures to add more, management begins to make mistakes. At the same time, the inevitable costs of being part of a diversified company take their toll and unit performance slides while the whole company's ROI turns downward. Eventually, a new management team is installed that initiates wholesale divestments and pares down the company to its core businesses. The experiences of Gulf & Western, Consolidated Foods (now Sara Lee), and ITT are just a few comparatively recent examples. Reflecting these realities, the U.S. capital markets today reward companies that follow the portfolio management model with a "conglomerate discount"; they value the whole less than the sum of the parts.

In developing countries, where large companies are few, capital markets are undeveloped, and professional management is scarce, portfolio management still works. But it is no longer a valid model for corporate strategy in advanced economies. Nevertheless, the technique is in the limelight today in the United Kingdom, where it is supported so far by a newly energized stock market eager for excitement. But this enthusiasm will wane – as well it should. Portfolio management is no way to conduct corporate strategy.

Restructuring

Unlike its passive role as a portfolio manager, when it serves as banker and reviewer, a company that bases its strategy on restructuring becomes an active restructurer of business units. The new businesses are not necessarily related to existing units. All that is necessary is unrealized potential.

The restructuring strategy seeks out undeveloped, sick, or threatened organizations or industries on the threshold of significant change. The parent intervenes, frequently changing the unit management team, shifting strategy, or infusing the company with new technology. Then it may make follow-up acquisitions to build a critical mass and sell off unneeded or unconnected parts and thereby reduce the effective acquisition cost. The result is a strengthened company or a transformed industry. As a coda, the parent sells off the stronger unit once results are clear because the parent is no longer adding value and top management decides that its attention should be directed elsewhere. (See the insert "An Uncanny British Restructurer" for an example of restructuring.)

A strong sense of corporate identity is as important as slavish adherence to business unit financial results.

When well implemented, the restructuring concept is sound, for it passes the three tests of successful diversification. The restructurer meets the cost-of-entry test through the types of company it acquires. It limits acquisition premiums by buying companies with problems and lackluster images or by buying into industries with as yet unforeseen potential. Intervention by the corporation clearly meets the better-off test. Provided that the target industries are structurally attractive, the restructuring model can create enormous shareholder value. Some restructuring companies are Loew's, BTR, and General Cinema. Ironically, many of today's restructurers are profiting from yesterday's portfolio management strategies.

To work, the restructuring strategy requires a corporate management team with the insight to spot undervalued companies or positions in industries ripe for transformation. The same insight is necessary to actually turn the units around even though they are in new and unfamiliar businesses.

These requirements expose the restructurer to considerable risk and usually limit the time in which the company can succeed at the strategy. The most skillful proponents understand this problem, recognize their mistakes, and move decisively to dispose of them. The best companies realize they are not just acquiring companies but restructuring an industry. Unless they can integrate the acquisitions to create a whole new strategic position, they are just portfolio managers in disguise. Another important difficulty surfaces if so many other companies join the action that they deplete the pool of suitable candidates and bid their prices up.

Perhaps the greatest pitfall, however, is that companies find it very hard to dispose of business units once they are restructured and performing well.

Exhibit IV   Concepts of corporate strategy

	Portfolio management	Restructuring	Transferring skills	Sharing activities
Strategic prerequisites	Superior insight into identifying and acquiring undervalued companies

Willingness to sell off losers quickly or to opportunistically divest good performers when buyers are willing to pay large premiums

Broad guidelines for and constraints on the types of units in the portfolio so that senior management can play the review role effectively

A private company or undeveloped capital markets

Ability to shift away from portfolio management as the capital markets get more efficient or the company gets unwieldy | Superior insight into identifying restructuring opportunities

Willingness and capability to intervene to transform acquired units

Broad similarities among the units in the portfolio

Willingness to cut losses by selling off units where restructuring proves unfeasible

Willingness to sell units when restructuring is complete, the results are clear, and market conditions are favorable | Proprietary skills in activities important to competitive advantage in target industries

Ability to accomplish the transfer of skills among units on an ongoing basis

Acquisitions of beachhead positions in new industries as a base | Activities in existing units that can be shared with new business units to gain competitive advantage

Benefits of sharing that outweigh the costs

Both start-ups and acquisitions as entry vehicles

Ability to overcome organizational resistance to business unit collaboration |
| **Organizational prerequisites** | Autonomous business units

A very small, low-cost, corporate staff

Incentives based largely on business unit results | Autonomous business units

A corporate organization with the talent and resources to oversee the turnarounds and strategic repositionings of acquired units

Incentives based largely on acquired units' results | Largely autonomous but collaborative business units

High-level corporate staff members who see their role primarily as integrators

Cross-business-unit committees, task forces, and other forums to serve as focal points for capturing and transferring skills

Objectives of line managers that include skills transfer

Incentives based in part on corporate results | Strategic business units that are encouraged to share activities

An active strategic planning role at group, sector, and corporate levels

High-level corporate staff members who see their roles primarily as integrators

Incentives based heavily on group and corporate results |
| **Common pitfalls** | Pursuing portfolio management in countries with efficient capital marketing and a developed pool of professional management talent

Ignoring the fact that industry structure is not attractive | Mistaking rapid growth or a "hot" industry as sufficient evidence of a restructuring opportunity

Lacking the resolve or resources to take on troubled situations and to intervene in management

Ignoring the fact that industry structure is not attractive

Paying lip service to restructuring but actually practicing passive portfolio management | Mistaking similarity or comfort with new businesses as sufficient basis for diversification

Providing no practical ways for skills transfer to occur

Ignoring the fact that industry structure is not attractive | Sharing for its own sake rather than because it leads to competitive advantage

Assuming sharing will occur naturally without senior management playing an active role

Ignoring the fact that industry structure is not attractive |

Human nature fights economic rationale. Size supplants shareholder value as the corporate goal. The company does not sell a unit even though the company no longer adds value to the unit. While the transformed units would be better off in another company that had related businesses, the restructuring company instead retains them. Gradually, it becomes a portfolio manager. The parent company's ROI declines as the need for reinvestment in the units and normal business risks eventually offset restructuring's one-shot gain. The perceived need to keep growing intensifies the pace of acquisition; errors result and standards fall. The restructuring company turns into a conglomerate with returns that only equal the average of all industries at best.

Transferring skills

The purpose of the first two concepts of corporate strategy is to create value through a company's relationship with each autonomous unit. The corporation's role is to be a selector, a banker, and an intervenor.

The last two concepts exploit the interrelationships between businesses. In articulating them, however, one comes face-to-face with the often ill-defined concept of synergy. If you believe the text of the countless corporate annual reports, just about anything is related to just about anything else! But imagined synergy is much more common than real synergy. GM's purchase of Hughes Aircraft simply because cars were going electronic and Hughes was an electronics concern demonstrates the folly of paper synergy. Such corporate relatedness is an ex post facto rationalization of a diversification undertaken for other reasons.

Portfolio management is no way to conduct corporate strategy.

Even synergy that is clearly defined often fails to materialize. Instead of cooperating, business units often compete. A company that can define the synergies it is pursuing still faces significant organizational impediments in achieving them.

But the need to capture the benefits of relationships between businesses has never been more important. Technological and competitive developments already link many businesses and are creating new possibilities for competitive advantage. In such sectors as financial services, computing, office equipment, entertainment, and health care, interrelationships among previously distinct businesses are perhaps the central concern of strategy.

To understand the role of relatedness in corporate strategy, we must give new meaning to this often ill-defined idea. I have identified a good way to start—the value chain.[5] Every business unit is a collection of discrete activities ranging from sales to accounting that allow it to compete. I call them value activities. It is at this level, not in the company as a whole, that the unit achieves competitive advantage.

I group these activities in nine categories. *Primary* activities create the product or service, deliver and market it, and provide after-sale support. The categories of primary activities are inbound logistics, operations, outbound logistics, marketing and sales, and service. *Support* activities provide the input and infrastructure that allow the primary activities to take place. The categories are company infrastructure, human resource management, technology development, and procurement.

The value chain defines the two types of interrelationships that may create synergy. The first is a company's ability to transfer skills or expertise among similar value chains. The second is the ability to share activities. Two business units, for example, can share the same sales force or logistics network.

The value chain helps expose the last two (and most important) concepts of corporate strategy. The transfer of skills among business units in the diversified company is the basis for one concept. While each business unit has a separate value chain, knowledge about how to perform activities is transferred among the units. For example, a toiletries business unit, expert in the marketing of convenience products, transmits ideas on new positioning concepts, promotional techniques, and packaging possibilities to a newly acquired unit that sells cough syrup. Newly entered industries can benefit from the expertise of existing units and vice versa.

These opportunities arise when business units have similar buyers or channels, similar value activities like government relations or procurement, similarities in the broad configuration of the value chain (for example, managing a multisite service organization), or the same strategic concept (for example, low cost). Even though the units operate separately, such similarities allow the sharing of knowledge.

Of course, some similarities are common; one can imagine them at some level between almost any pair of businesses. Countless companies have fallen into the trap of diversifying too readily because of similarities; mere similarity is not enough.

Transferring skills leads to competitive advantage only if the similarities among businesses meet three conditions:

1   The activities involved in the businesses are similar enough that sharing expertise is meaningful. Broad similarities (marketing intensiveness, for example, or a common core process technology such as bending metal) are not a sufficient basis for diversification. The resulting ability to transfer skills is likely to have little impact on competitive advantage.

2   The transfer of skills involves activities important to competitive advantage. Transferring skills in peripheral activities such as government relations or real estate in consumer goods units may be beneficial but is not a basis for diversification.

3   The skills transferred represent a significant source of competitive advantage for the receiving unit. The expertise or skills to be transferred are both advanced and proprietary enough to be beyond the capabilities of competitors.

The transfer of skills is an active process that significantly changes the strategy or operations of the receiving unit. The prospect for change must be specific and identifiable. Almost guaranteeing that no shareholder value will be created, too many companies

An uncanny British restructurer

Hanson Trust, on its way to becoming Britain's largest company, is one of several skillful followers of the restructuring concept. A conglomerate with units in many industries, Hanson might seem on the surface a portfolio manager. In fact, Hanson and one or two other conglomerates have a much more effective corporate strategy. Hanson has acquired companies such as London Brick, Ever Ready Batteries, and SCM, which the city of London rather disdainfully calls "low tech."

Although a mature company suffering from low growth, the typical Hanson target is not just in any industry; it has an attractive structure. Its customer and supplier power is low and rivalry with competitors moderate. The target is a market leader, rich in assets but formerly poor in management. Hanson pays little of the present value of future cash flow out in an acquisition premium and reduces purchase price even further by aggressively selling off businesses that it cannot improve. In this way, it recoups just over a third of the cost of a typical acquisition during the first six months of ownership. Imperial Group's plush properties in London lasted barely two months under Hanson ownership, while Hanson's recent sale of Courage Breweries to Elders recouped £1.4 billion of the original £2.1 billion acquisition price of Imperial Group.

Like the best restructurers, Hanson approaches each unit with a modus operandi that it has perfected through repetition.

Hanson emphasizes low costs and tight financial controls. It has cut an average of 25% of labor costs out of acquired companies, slashed fixed overheads, and tightened capital expenditures. To reinforce its strategy of keeping costs low, Hanson carves out detailed one-year financial budgets with divisional managers and (through generous use of performance-related bonuses and share option schemes) gives them incentive to deliver the goods.

It's too early to tell whether Hanson will adhere to the last tenet of restructuring – selling turned-around units once the results are clear. If it succumbs to the allure of bigness, Hanson may take the course of the failed U.S. conglomerates.

---

are satisfied with vague prospects or faint hopes that skills will transfer. The transfer of skills does not happen by accident or by osmosis. The company will have to reassign critical personnel, even on a permanent basis, and the participation and support of high-level management in skills transfer is essential. Many companies have been defeated at skills transfer because they have not provided their business units with any incentives to participate.

Transferring skills meets the tests of diversification if the company truly mobilizes proprietary expertise across units. This makes certain the company can offset the acquisition premium or lower the cost of overcoming entry barriers.

The industries the company chooses for diversification must pass the attractiveness test. Even a close fit that reflects opportunities to transfer skills may not overcome poor industry structure. Opportunities to transfer skills, however, may help the company transform the structures of newly entered industries and send them in favorable directions.

The transfer of skills can be one-time or ongoing. If the company exhausts opportunities to infuse new expertise into a unit after the initial post-acquisition period, the unit should ultimately be sold. The corporation is no longer creating shareholder value. Few companies have grasped this point, however, and many gradually suffer mediocre returns. Yet a company diversified into well-chosen businesses can transfer skills eventually in many directions. If corporate management conceives of its role in this way and creates appropriate organizational mechanisms to facilitate cross-unit interchange, the opportunities to share expertise will be meaningful.

By using both acquisitions and internal development, companies can build a transfer-of-skills strategy. The presence of a strong base of skills sometimes creates the possibility for internal entry instead of the acquisition of a going concern. Successful diversifiers that employ the concept of skills transfer may, however, often acquire a company in the target industry as a beachhead and then build on it with their internal expertise. By doing so, they can reduce some of the risks of internal entry and speed up the process. Two companies that have diversified using the transfer-of-skills concept are 3M and Pepsico.

Sharing activities

The fourth concept of corporate strategy is based on sharing activities in the value chains among business units. Procter & Gamble, for example, employs a common physical distribution system and sales force in both paper towels and disposable diapers. McKesson, a leading distribution company, will handle such diverse lines as pharmaceuticals and liquor through superwarehouses.

The ability to share activities is a potent basis for corporate strategy because sharing often enhances competitive advantage by lowering cost or raising differentiation. But not all sharing leads to competitive advantage, and companies can encounter deep organizational resistance to even beneficial sharing possibilities. These hard truths have led many companies to reject synergy prematurely and retreat to the false simplicity of portfolio management.

A cost-benefit analysis of prospective sharing opportunities can determine whether synergy is possible. Sharing can lower costs if it achieves economies of scale, boosts the efficiency of utilization, or helps a company move more rapidly down the learning curve. The costs of General Electric's advertising, sales, and after-sales service activities in major appliances are low because they are spread over a wide range of appliance products. Sharing can also enhance the potential for differentiation. A shared order-processing system, for instance, may allow new features and services that a buyer will value. Sharing can also reduce the cost of differentiation. A shared service network, for example, may make more advanced, remote servicing technology economically feasible. Often, sharing will allow an activity to be wholly reconfigured in ways that can dramatically raise competitive advantage.

Sharing must involve activities that are significant to competitive advantage, not just any activity. P&G's distribution system is such an instance in the diaper and paper towel business, where products are bulky and costly to ship. Conversely, diversification based on the opportunities to share only corporate overhead is rarely, if ever, appropriate.

Sharing activities inevitably involves costs that the benefits must outweigh. One cost is the greater coordination required to manage a shared activity. More important is the need to compromise the design or performance of an activity so that it can be shared. A salesperson handling the products of two business units, for example, must operate in a way that is usually not what either unit would choose were it independent. And if compromise greatly erodes the unit's effectiveness, then sharing may reduce rather than enhance competitive advantage.

Many companies have only superficially identified their potential for sharing. Companies also merge activities without consideration of whether they are sensitive to economies of scale. When they are not, the coordination costs kill the benefits. Companies compound such errors by not identifying costs of sharing in advance, when steps can be taken to minimize them. Costs of compromise can frequently be mitigated by redesigning the activity for sharing. The shared salesperson, for example, can be provided with a remote computer terminal to boost productivity and provide more customer information. Jamming business units together without such thinking exacerbates the costs of sharing.

Despite such pitfalls, opportunities to gain advantage from sharing activities have proliferated because of momentous developments in technology, deregulation, and competition. The infusion of electronics and information systems into many industries creates new opportunities to link businesses. The corporate strategy of sharing can involve both acquisition and internal development. Internal development is of-

Adding value with hospitality

Marriott began in the restaurant business in Washington, D.C. Because its customers often ordered takeouts on the way to the national airport, Marriott eventually entered airline catering. From there, it jumped into food service management for institutions. Marriott then began broadening its base of family restaurants and entered the hotel industry. More recently, it has moved into restaurants, snack bars, and merchandise shops in airport terminals and into gourmet restaurants. In addition, Marriott has branched out from its hotel business into cruise ships, theme parks, wholesale travel agencies, budget motels, and retirement centers.

Marriott's diversification has exploited well-developed skills in food service and hospitality. Marriott's kitchens prepare food according to more than 6,000 standardized recipe cards; hotel procedures are also standardized and painstakingly documented in elaborate manuals. Marriott shares a number of important activities across units. A shared procurement and distribution system for food serves all Marriott units through nine regional procurement centers. As a result, Marriott earns 50% higher margins on food service than any other hotel company. Marriott also has a fully integrated real estate unit that brings corporatewide power to bear on site acquisitions as well as on the designing and building of all Marriott locations.

Marriott's diversification strategy balances acquisitions and start-ups. Start-ups or small acquisitions are used for initial entry, depending on how close the opportunities for sharing are. To expand its geographic base, Marriott acquires companies and then disposes of the parts that do not fit.

Apart from this success, it is important to note that Marriott has divested 36% of both its acquisitions and its start-ups. While this is an above-average record, Marriott's mistakes are quite illuminating. Marriott has largely failed in diversifying into gourmet restaurants, theme parks, cruise ships, and wholesale travel agencies. In the first three businesses, Marriott discovered it could not transfer skills despite apparent similarities. Standardized menus did not work well in gourmet restaurants. Running cruise ships and theme parks was based more on entertainment and pizzazz than the carefully disciplined management of hotels and midprice restaurants. The wholesale travel agencies were ill fated from the start because Marriott had to compete with an important customer for its hotels and had no proprietary skills or opportunities to share with which to add value.

ten possible because the corporation can bring to bear clear resources in launching a new unit. Start-ups are less difficult to integrate than acquisitions. Companies using the shared-activities concept can also make acquisitions as beachhead landings into a new industry and then integrate the units through sharing with other units. Prime examples of companies that have diversified via using shared activities include P&G, Du Pont, and IBM. The fields into which each has diversified are a cluster of tightly related units. Marriott illustrates both successes and failures in sharing activities over time. (See the insert "Adding Value with Hospitality.")

Following the shared-activities model requires an organizational context in which business unit collaboration is encouraged and reinforced. Highly autonomous business units are inimical to such collaboration. The company must put into place a variety of what I call horizontal mechanisms – a strong sense of corporate identity, a clear corporate mission statement that emphasizes the importance of integrating business unit strategies, an incentive system that rewards more than just business unit results, cross-business-unit task forces, and other methods of integrating.

A corporate strategy based on shared activities clearly meets the better-off test because business units gain ongoing tangible advantages from others within the corporation. It also meets the cost-of-entry test by reducing the expense of surmounting the barriers to internal entry. Other bids for acquisitions that do not share opportunities will have lower reservation prices. Even widespread opportunities for sharing activities do not allow a company to suspend the attractiveness test, however. Many diversifiers have made the critical mistake of equating the close fit of a target industry with attractive diversification. Target industries must pass the strict requirement test of having an attractive structure as well as a close fit in opportunities if diversification is to ultimately succeed.

Choosing a corporate strategy

Each concept of corporate strategy allows the diversified company to create shareholder value in a different way. Companies can succeed with any of the concepts if they clearly define the corporation's role and objectives, have the skills necessary for meeting the concept's prerequisites, organize themselves to manage diversity in a way that fits the strategy, and find themselves in an appropriate capital market environment. The caveat is that portfolio management is only sensible in limited circumstances.

A company's choice of corporate strategy is partly a legacy of its past. If its business units are in unattractive industries, the company must start from scratch. If the company has few truly proprietary skills or activities it can share in related diversification, then its initial diversification must rely on other concepts. Yet corporate strategy should not be a once-and-for-all choice but a vision that can evolve. A company should choose its long-term preferred concept and then proceed pragmatically toward it from its initial starting point.

Both the strategic logic and the experience of the companies I studied over the last decade suggest that a company will create shareholder value through diversification to a greater and greater extent as its strategy moves from portfolio management toward sharing activities. Because they do not rely on superior insight or other questionable assumptions about the company's capabilities, sharing activities and transferring skills offer the best avenues for value creation.

Sharing allows activities to change completely in ways that increase competitive advantage.

Each concept of corporate strategy is not mutually exclusive of those that come before, a potent advantage of the third and fourth concepts. A company can employ a restructuring strategy at the same time it transfers skills or shares activities. A strategy based on shared activities becomes more powerful if business units can also exchange skills. As the Marriott case illustrates, a company can often pursue the two strategies together and even incorporate some of the principles of restructuring with them. When it chooses industries in which to transfer skills or share activities, the company can also investigate the possibility of transforming the industry structure. When a company bases its strategy on interrelationships, it has a broader basis on which to create shareholder value than if it rests its entire strategy on transforming companies in unfamiliar industries.

My study supports the soundness of basing a corporate strategy on the transfer of skills or shared activities. The data on the sample companies' diversification programs illustrate some important characteristics of successful diversifiers. They have made a disproportionately low percentage of unrelated acquisitions, *unrelated* being defined as having no clear opportunity to transfer skills or share important activities (see *Exhibit III*). Even successful diversifiers such as 3M, IBM, and TRW have terrible records when they have strayed into unrelated acquisitions. Successful acquirers diversify into fields, each of which is related to many others. Procter & Gamble and IBM, for example, operate in 18 and 19 interrelated fields respectively and so enjoy numerous opportunities to transfer skills and share activities.

Companies with the best acquisition records tend to make heavier-than-average use of start-ups and joint ventures. Most companies shy away from modes of entry besides acquisition. My results cast doubt on the conventional wisdom regarding start-ups. *Exhibit III* demonstrates that while joint ventures are about as risky as acquisitions, start-ups are not. Moreover, successful companies often have very good records with start-up units, as 3M, P&G, Johnson & Johnson, IBM, and United Technologies illustrate. When a company has the internal strength to start up a unit, it can be safer and less costly to launch a company than to rely solely on an acquisition and then have to deal with the problem of integration. Japanese diversification histories support the soundness of start-up as an entry alternative.

My data also illustrate that none of the concepts of corporate strategy works when industry structure is poor or implementation is bad, no matter how related the industries are. Xerox acquired companies in related industries, but the businesses had poor structures and its skills were insufficient to provide enough competitive advantage to offset implementation problems.

An action program

To translate the principles of corporate strategy into successful diversification, a company must first take an objective look at its existing businesses and the value added by the corporation. Only through such an assessment can an understanding of good corporate strategy grow. That understanding should guide future diversification as well as the development of skills and activities with which to select further new businesses. The following action program provides a concrete approach to conducting such a review. A company can choose a corporate strategy by:

1   Identifying the interrelationships among already existing business units.

A company should begin to develop a corporate strategy by identifying all the opportunities it has to share activities or transfer skills in its existing portfolio of business units. The company will not only find ways to enhance the competitive advantage of existing units but also come upon several possible diversification avenues. The lack of meaningful interrelationships in the portfolio is an equally important finding, suggesting the need to justify the value added by the corporation or, alternately, a fundamental restructuring.

2   Selecting the core businesses that will be the foundation of the corporate strategy.

Successful diversification starts with an understanding of the core businesses that will serve as the basis for corporate strategy. Core businesses are those that are in an attractive industry, have the potential to achieve sustainable competitive advantage, have important interrelationships with other business units, and provide skills or activities that represent a base from which to diversify.

The company must first make certain its core businesses are on sound footing by upgrading management, internationalizing strategy, or improving technology. My study shows that geographic extensions of existing units, whether by acquisition, joint venture, or start-up, had a substantially lower divestment rate than diversification.

The company must then patiently dispose of the units that are not core businesses. Selling them will free resources that could be better deployed elsewhere. In some cases disposal implies immediate liquidation, while in others the company should dress up the units and wait for a propitious market or a particularly eager buyer.

3   Creating horizontal organizational mechanisms to facilitate interrelationships among the core businesses and lay the groundwork for future related diversification.

Top management can facilitate interrelationships by emphasizing cross-unit collaboration, grouping units organizationally and modifying incentives, and taking steps to build a strong sense of corporate identity.

4   Pursuing diversification opportunities that allow shared activities.

This concept of corporate strategy is the most compelling, provided a company's strategy passes all three tests. A company should inventory activities in existing business units that represent the strongest foundation for sharing, such as strong distribution channels or world-class technical facilities. These will in turn lead to potential new business areas. A company can use acquisitions as a beachhead or employ start-ups to exploit internal capabilities and minimize integrating problems.

5   Pursuing diversification through the transfer of skills if opportunities for sharing activities are limited or exhausted.

Companies can pursue this strategy through acquisition, although they may be able to use start-ups if their existing units have important skills they can readily transfer.

Such diversification is often riskier because of the tough conditions necessary for it to work. Given the uncertainties, a company should avoid diversifying on the basis of skills transfer alone. Rather it should also be viewed as a stepping-stone to subsequent diversification using shared activities. New industries should be chosen that will lead naturally to other businesses. The goal is to build a cluster of related and mutually reinforcing business units. The strategy's logic implies that the company should not set the rate of return standards for the initial foray into a new sector too high.

6   Pursuing a strategy of restructuring if this fits the skills of management or no good opportunities exist for forging corporate interrelationships.

When a company uncovers undermanaged companies and can deploy adequate management talent and resources to the acquired units, then it can use a restructuring strategy. The more developed the capital markets and the more active the market for companies, the more restructuring will require a patient search for that special opportunity rather than a headlong race to acquire as many bad apples as possible. Restructuring can be a permanent strategy, as it is with Loew's, or a way to build a group of businesses that supports a shift to another corporate strategy.

7   Paying dividends so that the shareholders can be the portfolio managers.

Paying dividends is better than destroying shareholder value through diversification based on shaky underpinnings. Tax considerations, which some companies cite to avoid dividends, are hardly legitimate reason to diversify if a company cannot demonstrate the capacity to do it profitably.

Creating a corporate theme

Defining a corporate theme is a good way to ensure that the corporation will create shareholder value. Having the right theme helps unite the efforts of business units and reinforces the ways they interrelate as well as guides the choice of new businesses to enter. NEC Corporation, with its "C&C" theme, provides a good example. NEC integrates its computer, semiconductor, telecommunications, and consumer electronics businesses by merging computers and communication.

It is all too easy to create a shallow corporate theme. CBS wanted to be an "entertainment company," for example, and built a group of businesses related to leisure time. It entered such industries as toys, crafts, musical instruments, sports teams, and hi-fi retailing. While this corporate theme sounded good, close listening revealed its hollow ring. None of these businesses had any significant opportunity to share activities or transfer skills among themselves or with CBS's traditional broadcasting and record businesses. They were all sold, often at significant losses, except for a few of CBS's publishing-related units. Saddled with the worst acquisition record in my study, CBS has eroded the shareholder value created through its strong performance in broadcasting and records.

Moving from competitive strategy to corporate strategy is the business equivalent of passing through the Bermuda Triangle. The failure of corporate strategy reflects the fact that most diversified companies have failed to think in terms of how they really add value. A corporate strategy that truly enhances the competitive advantage of each business unit is the best defense against the corporate raider. With a sharper focus on the tests of diversification and the explicit choice of a clear concept of corporate strategy, companies' diversification track records from now on can look a lot different.

Reprint 87307

References

1 The studies also show that sellers of companies capture a large fraction of the gains from merger. See Michael C. Jensen and Richard S. Ruback, "The Market for Corporate Control: The Scientific Evidence," *Journal of Financial Economics*, April 1983, p. 5, and Michael C. Jensen, "Takeovers: Folklore and Science," HBR November-December 1984, p. 109.

2 Some recent evidence also supports the conclusion that acquired companies often suffer eroding performance after acquisition. See Frederick M. Scherer, "Mergers, Sell-Offs and Managerial Behavior," in *The Economics of Strategic Planning*, ed. Lacy Glenn Thomas (Lexington, Mass.: Lexington Books, 1986), p. 143, and David A. Ravenscraft and Frederick M. Scherer, "Mergers and Managerial Performance," paper presented at the Conference on Takeovers and Contests for Corporate Control, Columbia Law School, 1985.

3 This observation has been made by a number of authors. See, for example, Malcolm S. Salter and Wolf A. Weinhold, *Diversification Through Acquisition* (New York: Free Press, 1979).

4 See Michael E. Porter, "How Competitive Forces Shape Strategy," HBR March-April 1979, p. 86.

5 Michael E. Porter, *Competitive Advantage* (New York: Free Press, 1985).

Author's note: The research for this article was done with the able assistance of my research associate Cheng G. Ong. Malcolm S. Salter, Andrall E. Pearson, A. Michael Keehner, and the Monitor Company also provided helpful comments.

*The information revolution
is transforming
the nature
of competition*

How information gives you competitive advantage

*Michael E. Porter and
Victor E. Millar*

It is hard to overestimate the strategic significance of the new information technology. This technology is transforming the nature of products, processes, companies, industries, and even competition itself. Until recently, most managers treated information technology as a support service and delegated it to EDP departments. Now, however, every company must understand the broad effects and implications of the new technology and how it can create substantial and sustainable competitive advantages.

The authors of this article provide a useful framework for analyzing the strategic significance of the new information technology. They show how and why the technology is changing the way companies operate internally as well as altering the relationships among companies and their suppliers, customers, and rivals. They go on to identify three specific ways that the technology affects competition: it alters industry structures, it supports cost and differentiation strategies, and it spawns entirely new businesses. They outline five steps to help managers assess the impact of the information revolution on their own companies.

Mr. Porter is professor of business administration at the Harvard Business School. He is the author of the new best-seller Competitive Advantage *(Free Press, 1985) and* Competitive Strategy *(Free Press, 1980), and he recently served on the Presidential Commission on Industrial Competitiveness.*

Mr. Millar is the managing partner for practice of Arthur Andersen & Co. and is responsible for the professional practices of the firm worldwide. He has worked extensively with executives to increase their understanding of information in the management function.

The information revolution is sweeping through our economy. No company can escape its effects. Dramatic reductions in the cost of obtaining, processing, and transmitting information are changing the way we do business.

Most general managers know that the revolution is under way, and few dispute its importance. As more and more of their time and investment capital is absorbed in information technology and its effects, executives have a growing awareness that the technology can no longer be the exclusive territory of EDP or IS departments. As they see their rivals use information for competitive advantage, these executives recognize the need to become directly involved in the management of the new technology. In the face of rapid change, however, they don't know how.

This article aims to help general managers respond to the challenges of the information revolution. How will advances in information technology affect competition and the sources of competitive advantage? What strategies should a company pursue to exploit the technology? What are the implications of actions that competitors may already have taken? Of the many opportunities for investment in information technology, which are the most urgent?

To answer these questions, managers must first understand that information technology is more than just computers. Today, information technology must be conceived of broadly to encompass the information that businesses create and use as well as a wide spectrum of increasingly convergent and linked technologies that process the information. In addition to computers, then, data recognition equipment, com-

Authors' note: We wish to thank Monitor Company and Arthur Andersen for their assistance in preparing this article. F. Warren McFarlan also provided valuable comments.

Editor's note: All references appear at the end of the article.

munications technologies, factory automation, and other hardware and services are involved.

The information revolution is affecting competition in three vital ways:

It changes industry structure and, in so doing, alters the rules of competition.

It creates competitive advantage by giving companies new ways to outperform their rivals.

It spawns whole new businesses, often from within a company's existing operations.

We discuss the reasons why information technology has acquired strategic significance and how it is affecting all businesses. We then describe how the new technology changes the nature of competition and how astute companies have exploited this. Finally, we outline a procedure managers can use to assess the role of information technology in their business and to help define investment priorities to turn the technology to their competitive advantage.

Strategic significance

Information technology is changing the way companies operate. It is affecting the entire process by which companies create their products. Furthermore, it is reshaping the product itself: the entire package of physical goods, services, and information companies provide to create value for their buyers.

An important concept that highlights the role of information technology in competition is the "value chain."[1] This concept divides a company's activities into the technologically and economically distinct activities it performs to do business. We call these "value activities." The value a company creates is measured by the amount that buyers are willing to pay for a product or service. A business is profitable if the value it creates exceeds the cost of performing the value activities. To gain competitive advantage over its rivals, a company must either perform these activities at a lower cost or perform them in a way that leads to differentiation and a premium price (more value).[2]

A company's value activities fall into nine generic categories (see *Exhibit I*). Primary activities are those involved in the physical creation of the product, its marketing and delivery to buyers, and its support and servicing after sale. Support activities provide the inputs and infrastructure that allow the primary activities to take place. Every activity employs purchased inputs, human resources, and a combination of technologies. Firm infrastructure, including such functions as general management, legal work, and accounting, supports the entire chain. Within each of these generic categories, a company will perform a number of discrete activities, depending on the particular business. Service, for example, frequently includes activities such as installation, repair, adjustment, upgrading, and parts inventory management.

A company's value chain is a system of interdependent activities, which are connected by linkages. Linkages exist when the way in which one activity is performed affects the cost or effectiveness of other activities. Linkages often create trade-offs in performing different activities that should be optimized. This optimization may require trade-offs. For example, a more costly product design and more expensive raw materials can reduce after-sale service costs. A company must resolve such trade-offs, in accordance with its strategy, to achieve competitive advantage.

Linkages also require activities to be coordinated. On-time delivery requires that operations, outbound logistics, and service activities (installation, for example) should function smoothly together. Good coordination allows on-time delivery without the need for costly inventory. Careful management of linkages is often a powerful source of competitive advantage because of the difficulty rivals have in perceiving them and in resolving trade-offs across organizational lines.

The value chain for a company in a particular industry is embedded in a larger stream of activities that we term the "value system" (see *Exhibit II*). The value system includes the value chains of suppliers, who provide inputs (such as raw materials, components, and purchased services) to the company's value chain. The company's product often passes through its channels' value chains on its way to the ultimate buyer. Finally, the product becomes a purchased input to the value chains of its buyers, who use it to perform one or more buyer activities.

Linkages not only connect value activities inside a company but also create interdependencies between its value chain and those of its suppliers and channels. A company can create competitive advantage by optimizing or coordinating these links to the outside. For example, a candy manufacturer may save processing steps by persuading its suppliers to deliver chocolate in liquid form rather than in molded bars. Just-in-time deliveries by the supplier may have the same effect. But the opportunities for savings through coordinating with suppliers and channels go far beyond logistics and order processing. The company, suppliers, and channels can all benefit through better recognition and exploitation of such linkages.

Competitive advantage in either cost or differentiation is a function of a company's value

Exhibit I   **The value chain**

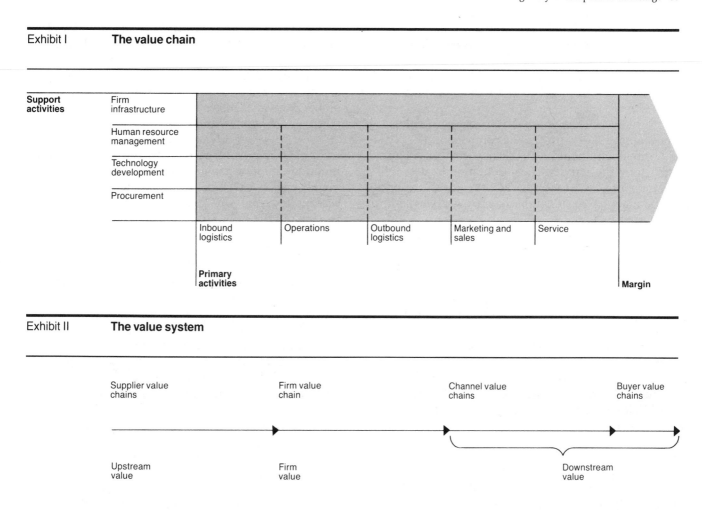

Exhibit II   **The value system**

chain. A company's cost position reflects the collective cost of performing all its value activities relative to rivals. Each value activity has cost drivers that determine the potential sources of a cost advantage. Similarly, a company's ability to differentiate itself reflects the contribution of each value activity toward fulfillment of buyer needs. Many of a company's activities – not just its physical product or service – contribute to differentiation. Buyer needs, in turn, depend not only on the impact of the company's product on the buyer but also on the company's other activities (for example, logistics or after-sale services).

In the search for competitive advantage, companies often differ in competitive scope – or the breadth of their activities. Competitive scope has four key dimensions: segment scope, vertical scope (degree of vertical integration), geographic scope, and industry scope (or the range of related industries in which the company competes).

Competitive scope is a powerful tool for creating competitive advantage. Broad scope can allow the company to exploit interrelationships between the value chains serving different industry segments, geographic areas, or related industries. For example, two business units may share one sales force to sell their products, or the units may coordinate the procurement of common components. Competing nationally or globally with a coordinated strategy can yield a competitive advantage over local or domestic rivals. By employing a broad vertical scope, a company can exploit the potential benefits of performing more activities internally rather than use outside suppliers.

By selecting a narrow scope, on the other hand, a company may be able to tailor the value chain to a particular target segment to achieve lower cost or differentiation. The competitive advantage of a narrow scope comes from customizing the value chain to best serve particular product varieties, buyers, or geographic regions. If the target segment has unusual needs, broad-scope competitors will not serve it well.

Transforming the value chain

Information technology is permeating the value chain at every point, transforming the way value activities are performed and the nature of the linkages among them. It also is affecting competitive scope and reshaping the way products meet buyer needs. These basic effects explain why information technology has acquired strategic significance and is different from the many other technologies businesses use.

Every value activity has both a physical and an information-processing component. The physical component includes all the physical tasks required to perform the activity. The information-processing component encompasses the steps required to capture, manipulate, and channel the data necessary to perform the activity.

Every value activity creates and uses information of some kind. A logistics activity, for example, uses information like scheduling promises, transportation rates, and production plans to ensure timely and cost-effective delivery. A service activity uses information about service requests to schedule calls and order parts, and generates information on product failures that a company can use to revise product designs and manufacturing methods.

An activity's physical and information-processing components may be simple or quite complex. Different activities require a different mix of the two components. For instance, metal stamping uses more physical processing than information processing; processing of insurance claims requires just the opposite balance.

For most of industrial history, technological progress principally affected the physical component of what businesses do. During the Industrial Revolution, companies achieved competitive advantage by substituting machines for human labor. Information processing at that time was mostly the result of human effort.

Now the pace of technological change is reversed. Information technology is advancing faster than technologies for physical processing. The costs of information storage, manipulation, and transmittal are falling rapidly and the boundaries of what is feasible in information processing are at the same time expanding. During the Industrial Revolution, the railroad cut the travel time from Boston, Massachusetts to Concord, New Hampshire from five days to four hours, a factor of 30.[3] But the advances in information technology are even greater. The cost of computer power relative to the cost of manual information processing is at least 8,000 times less expensive than the cost 30 years ago. Between 1958 and 1980 the time for one electronic operation fell by a factor of 80 million. Department of Defense studies show that the error rate in recording data through bar coding is 1 in 3,000,000, compared to 1 error in 300 manual data entries.[4]

This technological transformation is expanding the limits of what companies can do faster than managers can explore the opportunities. The information revolution affects all nine categories of value activity, from allowing computer-aided design in technology development to incorporating automation in warehouses (see *Exhibit III*). The new technology substitutes machines for human effort in information processing. Paper ledgers and rules of thumb have given way to computers.

Initially, companies used information technology mainly for accounting and record-keeping functions. In these applications, the computers automated repetitive clerical functions such as order processing. Today information technology is spreading throughout the value chain and is performing optimization and control functions as well as more judgmental executive functions. General Electric, for instance, uses a data base that includes the accumulated experience and (often intuitive) knowledge of its appliance service engineers to provide support to customers by phone.

Information technology is generating more data as a company performs its activities and is permitting it to collect or capture information that was not available before. Such technology also makes room for a more comprehensive analysis and use of the expanded data. The number of variables that a company can analyze or control has grown dramatically. Hunt-Wesson, for example, developed a computer model to aid it in studying distribution-center expansion and relocation issues. The model enabled the company to evaluate many more different variables, scenarios, and alternative strategies than had been possible before. Similarly, information technology helped Sulzer Brothers' engineers improve the design of diesel engines in ways that manual calculations could not.

Information technology is also transforming the physical processing component of activities. Computer-controlled machine tools are faster, more accurate, and more flexible in manufacturing than the older, manually operated machines. Schlumberger has developed an electronic device permitting engineers to measure the angle of a drill bit, the temperature of a rock, and other variables while drilling oil wells. The result: drilling time is reduced and some well-logging steps are eliminated. On the West Coast, some fishermen now use weather satellite data on ocean temperatures to identify promising fishing grounds. This practice greatly reduces the fishermen's steaming time and fuel costs.

Information technology not only affects how individual activities are performed but, through new information flows, it is also greatly enhancing a company's ability to exploit linkages between activities, both within and outside the company. The technology is creating new linkages between activities, and companies can now coordinate their actions more closely with those of their buyers and suppliers. For example, McKesson, the nation's largest drug distributor,

Exhibit III   **Information Technology permeates the value chain**

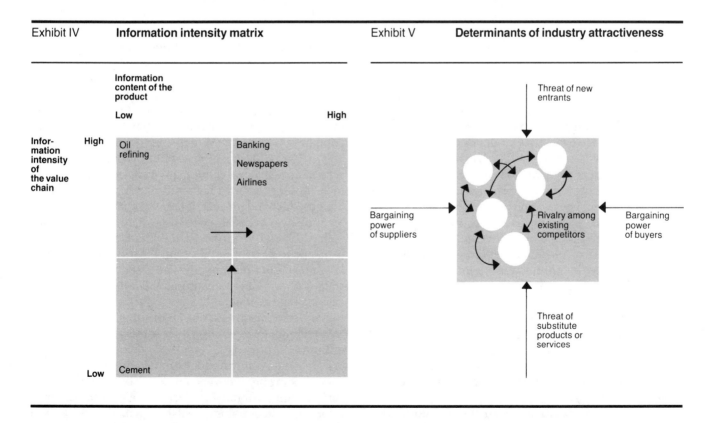

Support activities	Firm infrastructure	Planning models				
	Human resource management	Automated personnel scheduling				
	Technology development	Computer-aided design	Electronic market research			
	Procurement	On-line procurement of parts				
		Automated warehouse	Flexible manufacturing	Automated order processing	Telemarketing Remote terminals for salespersons	Remote servicing of equipment Computer scheduling and routing of repair trucks
		Inbound logistics	Operations	Outbound logistics	Marketing and sales	Service
	Primary activities					Margin

Exhibit IV   **Information intensity matrix**

Information content of the product

		Low	High
Information intensity of the value chain	High	Oil refining	Banking Newspapers Airlines
	Low	Cement	

Exhibit V   **Determinants of industry attractiveness**

Threat of new entrants

Bargaining power of suppliers

Rivalry among existing competitors

Bargaining power of buyers

Threat of substitute products or services

provides its drugstore customers with terminals. The company makes it so easy for clients to order, receive, and prepare invoices that the customers, in return, are willing to place larger orders. At the same time, McKesson has streamlined its order processing.

Finally, the new technology has a powerful effect on competitive scope. Information systems allow companies to coordinate value activities in far-flung geographic locations. (For example, Boeing engineers work on designs on-line with foreign suppliers.) Information technology is also creating many new interrelationships among businesses, expanding the scope of industries in which a company must compete to achieve competitive advantage.

So pervasive is the impact of information technology that it confronts executives with a tough problem: too much information. This problem creates new uses of information technology to store and analyze the flood of information available to executives.

Transforming the product

Most products have always had both a physical and an information component. The latter, broadly defined, is everything that the buyer needs to know to obtain the product and use it to achieve the desired result. That is, a product includes information about its characteristics and how it should be used and supported. For example, convenient, accessible information on maintenance and service procedures is an important buyer criterion in consumer appliances.

Historically, a product's physical component has been more important than its information component. The new technology, however, makes it feasible to supply far more information along with the physical product. For example, General Electric's appliance service data base supports a consumer hotline that helps differentiate GE's service support from its rivals'. Similarly, some railroad and trucking companies offer up-to-the-minute information on the whereabouts of shippers' freight, which improves coordination between shippers and the railroad. The new technology is also making it increasingly possible to offer products with no physical component at all. Compustat's customers have access to corporate financial data filed with the Securities and Exchange Commission, and many companies have sprung up to perform energy use analyses of buildings.

Many products also process information in their normal functioning. A dishwasher, for example, requires a control system that directs the various components of the unit through the washing cycle and displays the process to the user. The new information technology is enhancing product performance and is making it easier to boost a product's information content. Electronic control of the automobile, for example, is becoming more visible in dashboard displays, talking dashboards, diagnostic messages, and the like.

There is an unmistakable trend toward expanding the information content in products. This component, combined with changes in companies' value chains, underscores the increasingly strategic role of information technology. There are no longer mature industries; rather, there are mature ways of doing business.

Direction & pace of change

Although a trend toward information intensity in companies and products is evident, the role and importance of the technology differs in each industry. Banking and insurance, for example, have always been information intensive. Such industries were naturally among the first and most enthusiastic users of data processing. On the other hand, physical processing will continue to dominate in industries that produce, say, cement, despite increased information processing in such businesses.

Exhibit IV, which relates information intensity in the value chain to information content in the product, illuminates the differences in the role and intensity of information among various industries. The banking and newspaper industries have a high information-technology content in both product and process. The oil-refining industry has a high use of information in the refining process but a relatively low information content in the product dimension.

Because of the falling cost and growing capacity of the new technology, many industries seem to be moving toward a higher information content in both product and process. It should be emphasized that technology will continue to improve rapidly. The cost of hardware will continue to drop, and managers will continue to distribute the technology among even the lower levels of the company. The cost of developing software, now a key constraint, will fall as more packages become available that are easily tailored to customers' circumstances. The applications of information technology that companies are using today are only a beginning.

Information technology is not only transforming products and processes but also the nature of competition itself. Despite the growing use of information technology, industries will always differ in their position in *Exhibit IV* and their pace of change.

Changing the nature of competition

After surveying a wide range of industries, we find that information technology is changing the rules of competition in three ways. First, advances in information technology are changing the industry structure. Second, information technology is an increasingly important lever that companies can use to create competitive advantage. A company's search for competitive advantage through information technology often also spreads to affect industry structure as competitors imitate the leader's strategic innovations. Finally, the information revolution is spawning completely new businesses. These three effects are critical for understanding the impact of information technology on a particular industry and for formulating effective strategic responses.

Changing industry structure

The structure of an industry is embodied in five competitive forces that collectively determine industry profitability: the power of buyers, the power of suppliers, the threat of new entrants, the threat of substitute products, and the rivalry among existing competitors (see *Exhibit V*). The collective strength of the five forces varies from industry to industry, as does average profitability. The strength of each of the five forces can also change, either improving or eroding the attractiveness of an industry.[5]

Information technology can alter each of the five competitive forces and, hence, industry attractiveness as well. The technology is unfreezing the structure of many industries, creating the need and opportunity for change. For example:

☐ Information technology increases the power of buyers in industries assembling purchased components. Automated bills for materials and vendor quotation files make it easier for buyers to evaluate sources of materials and make-or-buy decisions.

☐ Information technologies requiring large investments in complex software have raised the barriers to entry. For example, banks competing in cash management services for corporate clients now need advanced software to give customers on-line account information. These banks may also need to invest in improved computer hardware and other facilities.

☐ Flexible computer-aided design and manufacturing systems have influenced the threat of

Information technology and industry structure

Buyer power	Videotex home shopping services, such as Comp-U-Card, increase buyers' information. Buyers use their personal computers to browse through electronic catalogs and compare prices and product specifications. Customers can make purchases at any hour at prices typically 25% to 30% below suggested retail levels. Comp-U-Card is growing quickly: revenues have quintupled in two years to $9.5 million and membership is now 15,000. According to some projections, by the mid-1990s, 75% of U.S. households will have access to such services.
Buyer power	Shelternet, an electronic information exchange offered by First Boston Corporation, allows real estate brokers to determine quickly and easily what mortgage packages are available and whether the buyer will qualify for financing. This improves the position of both brokers and homebuyers in shopping for mortgages. The parties can make preliminary commitments within 30 minutes.
Substitution	Electronic data bases, such as NEXIS, are substituting for library research and consulting firms. NEXIS subscribers can quickly search the full text of any article in 225 periodicals. Users drastically reduce the time spent in literature searches. In addition, the buyer avoids the cost of journal subscriptions and pays only for the information required.

substitution in many industries by making it quicker, easier, and cheaper to incorporate enhanced features into products.

☐ The automation of order processing and customer billing has increased rivalry in many distribution industries. The new technology raises fixed costs at the same time as it displaces people. As a result, distributors must often fight harder for incremental volume.

Industries such as airlines, financial services, distribution, and information suppliers (see the upper right-hand corner of *Exhibit IV*) have felt these effects so far.[6] (See the insert, "Information Technology and Industry Structure," for more examples.)

Information technology has had a particularly strong impact on bargaining relationships between suppliers and buyers since it affects the linkages between companies and their suppliers, channels, and buyers. Information systems that cross company lines are becoming common. In some cases, the boundaries of industries themselves have changed.[7]

Systems that connect buyers and suppliers are spreading. Xerox gives manufacturing data to suppliers electronically to help them deliver materials. To speed up order entry, Westinghouse Electric Supply Company and American Hospital Supply have furnished their customers with terminals. Among other things, many systems raise the costs of switching to a new partner because of the disruption and retraining required. These systems tend to tie companies more closely to their buyers and suppliers.

Information technology is altering the relationship among scale, automation, and flexibility with potentially profound consequences. Large-scale production is no longer essential to achieve automation. As a result, entry barriers in a number of industries are falling.

At the same time, automation no longer necessarily leads to inflexibility. For example, General Electric rebuilt its Erie locomotive facility as a large-scale yet flexible factory using computers to store all design and manufacturing data. Ten types of motor frames can be accommodated without manual adjustments to the machines. After installation of a "smart" manufacturing system, BMW can build customized cars (each with its own tailored gearbox, transmission system, interior, and other features) on the normal assembly line. Automation and flexibility are achieved simultaneously, a pairing that changes the pattern of rivalry among competitors.

The increasing flexibility in performing many value activities combined with the falling costs of designing products has triggered an avalanche of opportunities to customize and to serve small market niches. Computer-aided design capability not only reduces the cost of designing new products but also dramatically reduces the cost of modifying or adding features to existing products. The cost of tailoring products to market segments is falling, again affecting the pattern of industry rivalry.

While managers can use information technology to improve their industry structure, the technology also has the potential to destroy that structure. For example, information systems now permit the airline industry to alter fares frequently and to charge many different fares between any two points. At the same time, however, the technology makes the flight and fare schedules more readily available and allows travel agents and individuals to shop around quickly for the lowest fare. The result is a lower fare structure than might otherwise exist. Information technology has made a number of professional service industries less attractive by reducing personal interaction and making service more of a commodity. Managers must look carefully at the structural implications of the new technology to realize its advantages or to be prepared for its consequences.

Creating competitive advantage

In any company, information technology has a powerful effect on competitive advantage in either cost or differentiation. The technology affects value activities themselves or allows companies to gain competitive advantage by exploiting changes in competitive scope.

Lowering cost. As we have seen, information technology can alter a company's costs in any part of the value chain.[8] The technology's historical impact on cost was confined to activities in which repetitive information processing played a large part. These limits no longer exist, however. Even activities like assembly that mainly involve physical processing now have a large information-processing component.

Canon, for example, built a low-cost copier assembly process around an automated parts-selection and materials-handling system. Assembly workers have bins containing all the parts needed for the particular copier. Canon's success with this system derives from the software that controls parts inventory and selection. In insurance brokerage, a number of insurance companies usually participate in underwriting a contract. The costs of documenting each company's participation are high. Now a computer model can optimize (and often reduce) the number of insurers per contract, lowering the broker's total cost. In garment production, equipment such as automated pattern drawers, fabric cutters, and systems for delivering cloth to the final sewing station have reduced the labor time for manufacturing by up to 50%. (See the insert, "Aim: A Competitive Edge," for further examples.)

In addition to playing a direct role in cost, information technology often alters the cost drivers of activities in ways that can improve (or erode) a company's relative cost position. For example, Louisiana Oil & Tire has taken all ten of its salespeople off the road and made them into telemarketers. As a result, sales expenses have fallen by 10% and sales volume has doubled. However, the move has made the national scale of operations the key determinant of the cost of selling, rather than regional scale.

Aim:
a competitive edge

Lowering Cost	Casinos spend up to 20% of revenues on complimentary services for high rollers. One assignment for pit bosses has always been to keep an eye out for the big spenders. Now, however, many casinos have developed computer systems to analyze data on customers. Caesar's Palace lowered its complimentary budget more than 20% by developing a player-rating system for more accurate identification of big spenders.
Enhancing Differentiation	American Express has developed differentiated travel services for corporate customers through the use of information technology. The services include arranging travel and close monitoring of individual expenses. Computers search for the lowest airplane fares, track travel expenses for each cardholder, and issue monthly statements.

Enhancing differentiation. The impact of information technology on differentiation strategies is equally dramatic. As noted earlier, the role of a company and its product in the buyer's value chain is the key determinant of differentiation. The new information technology makes it possible to customize products. Using automation, for instance, Sulzer Brothers has increased from five to eight the number of cylinder bore sizes of new low-speed marine diesel engines. Shipowners now choose an engine that is more precisely suited to their needs and thereby recoup significant fuel savings. Similarly, Digital Equipment's artificial intelligence system, XCON, uses decision rules to develop custom computer configurations. This dramatically reduces the time required to fill orders and increases accuracy—which enhances Digital's image as a quality provider.

By bundling more information with the physical product package sold to the buyer, the new technology affects a company's ability to differentiate itself. For example, a magazine distributor offers retailers processing credits for unsold items more efficiently than its competitors. Similarly, the embedding of information systems in the physical product itself is an increasingly powerful way to distinguish it from competing goods.

Changing competitive scope. Information technology can alter the relationship between competitive scope and competitive advantage. The technology increases a company's ability to coordinate its activities regionally, nationally, and globally. It can unlock the power of broader geographic scope to create competitive advantage. Consider the newspaper industry. Dow Jones, publisher of the *Wall Street Journal,* pioneered the page transmission technology that links its 17 U.S. printing plants to produce a truly national newspaper. Such advances in communication plants have also made it possible to move toward a global strategy. Dow Jones has started the *Asian Wall Street Journal* and the *Wall Street Journal-European Edition* and shares much of the editorial content while printing the papers in plants all over the world.

The information revolution is creating interrelationships among industries that were previously separate. The merging of computer and telecommunications technologies is an important example. This convergence has profound effects on the structure of both industries. For example, AT&T is using its position in telecommunications as a staging point for entry into the computer industry. IBM, which recently acquired Rolm, the telecommunications equipment manufacturer, is now joining the competition from the other direction. Information technology is also at the core of growing interrelationships in financial services, where the banking, insurance, and brokerage industries are merging, and in office equipment, where once distinct functions such as typing, photocopying, and data and voice communications can now be combined.

Broad-line companies are increasingly able to segment their offerings in ways that were previously feasible only for focused companies. In the trucking industry, Intermodal Transportation Services, Inc. of Cincinnati has completely changed its system for quoting prices. In the past, each local office set prices using manual procedures. Intermodal now uses microcomputers to link its offices to a center that calculates all prices. The new system gives the company the capacity to introduce a new pricing policy to offer discounts to national accounts, which place their orders from all over the country. Intermodal is tailoring its value chain to large national customers in a way that was previously impossible.

As information technology becomes more widespread, the opportunities to take advantage of a new competitive scope will only increase. The benefits of scope (and the achievement of linkages), however, can accrue only when the information technology spread throughout the organization can communicate. Completely decentralized organizational design and application of information technology will thwart these possibilities, because the information technology introduced in various parts of a company will not be compatible.

Spawning new businesses

The information revolution is giving birth to completely new industries in three distinct ways. First, it makes new businesses technologically feasible. For example, modern imaging and telecommunications technology blend to support new facsimile services such as Federal Express's Zapmail. Similarly, advances in microelectronics made personal computing possible. Services such as Merrill Lynch's Cash Management Account required new information technology to combine several financial products into one.

Second, information technology can also spawn new businesses by creating derived demand for new products. One example is Western Union's EasyLink service, a sophisticated, high-speed, data-communications network that allows personal computers, word processors, and other electronic devices to send messages to each other and to telex machines throughout the world. This service was not needed before the spread of information technology caused a demand for it.

Third, information technology creates new businesses within old ones. A company with information processing embedded in its value chain may have excess capacity or skills that can be sold outside. Sears took advantage of its skills in processing credit card accounts and of its massive scale to provide similar services to others. It sells credit-authorization and transaction-processing services to Phillips Petroleum and retail remittance-processing services to Mellon Bank. Similarly, a manufacturer of automotive parts, A.O. Smith, developed data-communications expertise to meet the needs of its traditional businesses. When a bank consortium went looking for a contractor to run a network of automated teller machines, A.O. Smith got the job. Eastman Kodak recently began offering long-distance telephone and data-transmission services through its internal telecommunications system. Where the information technology used in a company's value chain is sensitive to scale, a company may improve its overall competitive advantage by increasing the scale of information processing and lowering costs. By selling extra capacity outside, it is at the same time generating new revenue.

Companies also are increasingly able to create and sell to others information that is a by-product of their operations. National Benefit Life reportedly merged with American Can in part to gain access to data on the nine million customers of American Can's direct-mail retailing subsidiary. The use of bar-code scanners in supermarket retailing has turned grocery stores into market research labs. Retailers can run an ad in the morning newspaper and find out its effect by early afternoon. They can also sell this data to market research companies and to food processors.

Competing in the age of information

Senior executives can follow five steps to take advantage of opportunities that the information revolution has created.

1   **Assess information intensity.** A company's first task is to evaluate the existing and potential information intensity of the products and processes of its business units. To help managers accomplish this, we have developed some measures of the potential importance of information technology.

It is very likely that information technology will play a strategic role in an industry that is characterized by one or more of the following features:

☐   Potentially high information intensity in the value chain – a large number of suppliers or customers with whom the company deals directly, a product requiring a large quantity of information in selling, a product line with many distinct product varieties, a product composed of many parts, a large number of steps in a company's manufacturing process, a long cycle time from the initial order to the delivered product.

☐   Potentially high information intensity in the product – a product that mainly provides information, a product whose operation involves substantial information processing, a product whose use requires the buyer to process a lot of information, a product requiring especially high costs for buyer training, a product that has many alternative uses or is sold to a buyer with high information intensity in his or her own business.

These may help identify priority business units for investment in information technology. When selecting priority areas, remember the breadth of information technology – it involves more than simple computing.

2   **Determine the role of information technology in industry structure.** Managers should predict the likely impact of information technology on their industry's structure. They must examine how information technology might affect each of the five competitive forces. Not only is each force likely to change but

industry boundaries may change as well. Chances are that a new definition of the industry may be necessary.

Many companies are partly in control of the nature and pace of change in the industry structure. Companies have permanently altered the bases of competition in their favor in many industries through aggressive investments in information technology and have forced other companies to follow. Citibank, with its automated teller machines and transaction processing; American Airlines, with its computerized reservations system; and *USA Today,* with its newspaper page transmission to decentralized printing plants, are pioneers that have used information technology to alter industry structure. A company should understand how structural change is forcing it to respond and look for ways to lead change in the industry.

3   Identify and rank the ways in which information technology might create competitive advantage. The starting assumption must be that the technology is likely to affect every activity in the value chain. Equally important is the possibility that new linkages among activities are being made possible. By taking a careful look, managers can identify the value activities that are likely to be most affected in terms of cost and differentiation. Obviously, activities that represent a large proportion of cost or that are critical to differentiation bear closest scrutiny, particularly if they have a significant information-processing component. Activities with important links to other activities inside and outside the company are also critical. Executives must examine such activities for ways in which information technology can create sustainable competitive advantage.

In addition to taking a hard look at its value chain, a company should consider how information technology might allow a change in competitive scope. Can information technology help the company serve new segments? Will the flexibility of information technology allow broad-line competitors to invade areas that were once the province of niche competitors? Will information technology provide the leverage to expand the business globally? Can managers harness information technology to exploit interrelationships with other industries? Or, can the technology help a company create competitive advantage by narrowing its scope?

A fresh look at the company's product may also be in order:

Can the company bundle more information with the product?

Can the company embed information technology in it?

4   Investigate how information technology might spawn new businesses. Managers should consider opportunities to create new businesses from existing ones. Information technology is an increasingly important avenue for corporate diversification. Lockheed, for example, entered the data base business by perceiving an opportunity to use its spare computer capacity.

Identifying opportunities to spawn new businesses requires answering questions such as:

What information generated (or potentially generated) in the business could the company sell?

What information-processing capacity exists internally to start a new business?

Does information technology make it feasible to produce new items related to the company's product?

5   Develop a plan for taking advantage of information technology. The first four steps should lead to an action plan to capitalize on the information revolution. This action plan should rank the strategic investments necessary in hardware and software, and in new product development activities that reflect the increasing information content in products. Organizational changes that reflect the role that the technology plays in linking activities inside and outside the company are likely to be necessary.

The management of information technology can no longer be the sole province of the EDP department. Increasingly, companies must employ information technology with a sophisticated understanding of the requirements for competitive advantage. Organizations need to distribute the responsibility for systems development more widely in the organization. At the same time, general managers must be involved to ensure that cross-functional linkages, more possible to achieve with information technology, are exploited.

These changes do not mean that a central information-technology function should play an insignificant role. Rather than control information technology, however, an IS manager should coordinate the architecture and standards of the many applications throughout the organization, as well as provide assistance and coaching in systems development. Unless the numerous applications of information technology inside a company are compatible with each other, many benefits may be lost.

Information technology can help in the strategy implementation process. Reporting systems can track progress toward milestones and success factors. By using information systems, companies can measure their activities more precisely and help motivate managers to implement strategies successfully.[9]

The importance of the information revolution is not in dispute. The question is not whether information technology will have a significant impact on a company's competitive position; rather the question is when and how this impact will strike. Companies that anticipate the power of information technology will be in control of events. Companies that do not respond will be forced to accept changes that others initiate and will find themselves at a competitive disadvantage.

References

1 For more on the value chain concept, see Michael E. Porter, *Competitive Advantage* (New York: Free Press, 1985).

2 For a discussion of the two basic types of competitive advantage, see Michael E. Porter, *Competitive Strategy* (New York: Free Press, 1980), Chapter 2.

3 Alfred D. Chandler, Jr., *The Visible Hand* (Cambridge: Belknap Press of Harvard University Press, 1977), p. 86.

4 James L. McKenney and F. Warren McFarlan, "The Information Archipelago— Maps and Bridges," HBR September-October 1982, p. 109.

5 See Michael E. Porter, "How Competitive Forces Shape Strategy," HBR March-April 1979, p. 137.

6 See F. Warren McFarlan, "Information Technology Changes the Way You Compete," HBR May-June 1984, p. 98.

7 James I. Cash, Jr. and Benn R. Konsynski, "IS Redraws Competitive Boundaries," HBR March-April 1985, p. 134.

8 See Gregory L. Parsons, "Information Technology: A New Competitive Weapon," *Sloan Management Review*, Fall 1983, p. 3.

9 Victor E. Millar, "Decision-Oriented Information," *Datamation*, January 1984, p. 159.

Reprint 85415

Sears and the consensus

By the early 1920s, however, the "buyer for the American farmer" concept had begun to lose its relevance to economic and social realities. With the coming of the automobile and good roads, rural America rapidly became less isolated, and the kinds of merchandise of interest to the farm family came more and more to be the kinds of merchandise of interest to city dwellers as well. In this process, radio advertising also played a significant role. There was no longer a separately definable rural market with its own unique characteristics and needs; that market, and the previously distinct urban market, were homogenizing into a general American mass market.

The then managements of Sears and Ward's alike failed to grasp the significance of these new developments. They knew that their companies had problems; sales were increasingly difficult to get and profits were slipping.

Sears found the answer first—fortuitously. By bringing General Wood into the company in November of 1924, Julius Rosenwald acquired much more than the higher order of managerial skills he was seeking. He acquired a man who was capable of introducing a new entrepreneurial concept as fully responsive to the needs and opportunities of the times as Rosenwald's own had been to the needs and opportunities of a quarter-century earlier.

One of Wood's interesting personal traits was a fascination with census data. This had its origins during his years on the Canal, where good reading material—or, for that matter, any reading material—was scarce. The story is told that once, while confined to the infirmary with a minor ailment, the only thing Wood could find to read was the *Statistical Abstract of the United States*, which he began perusing simply to pass the time but soon came to study avidly. Whether or not the infirmary story is apocryphal, it is clear that in his Canal experience he acquired a taste for and an understanding of demographic and economic statistics that stayed with him for the rest of his life. During his mature years, there was a widely circulated myth (probably grounded in fact) that the *Statistical Abstract* was his favorite bedside reading. In any event, his keen grasp of major trends in American life was evident in his business planning and even ordinary conversation.

From
Shaping an American Institution: Robert E. Wood and Sears, Roebuck
by James C. Worthy
(Urbana and Chicago, Ill.: University of Illinois Press)
Copyright © 1984
Reprinted with the permission of the publisher.

How global companies win out

Three case studies illustrate the risks, the fight, and the ultimate reward of competing globally

Thomas Hout, Michael E. Porter, and Eileen Rudden

International competition. Citizens from most of the older industrialized countries have become obsessed with it since the first Japanese cars started selling well. Vulnerability has replaced invincibility as the word many would use to describe once firmly established international companies. But this disquiet obscures the steady achievements a number of corporations have made against competition from companies based outside their countries.

These companies rely on global strategies to succeed in today's world. That calls on a company to think of the world as one market instead of as a collection of national markets and sometimes requires decisions as unconventional as accepting projects with low ROIs because of their competitive payoff. An organization with such a global focus formulates long-term strategy for the company as a whole and then orchestrates the strategies of local subsidiaries accordingly.

The power of global strategies is illustrated here by the histories of three companies (one American, one European, and one Japanese) that have what the authors think it takes to win the new competitive game. These case studies should help managers decide whether a global strategy is appropriate for their companies.

Mr. Hout is a vice president in the Boston Consulting Group's Chicago office, dividing his time between clients in Chicago and Boston. He is the author of a number of articles on international competition, which have appeared in the Wall Street Journal *and* Foreign Affairs, *and is the coauthor of the book* Japanese Industrial Policy. *Mr. Porter is a professor at the Harvard Business School and is a leading authority in the field of competitive strategy. He is the author of numerous articles and of six books, including* Competitive Strategy: Techniques for Analyzing Industries and Competitors *(Free Press, 1980). He won the McKinsey Award for his article "How Competitive Forces Shape Strategy" (HBR March-April 1979). Ms. Rudden is a manager of the Boston Consulting Group's Boston office. This is Mr. Hout's and Ms. Rudden's first article for HBR.*

Hold that obituary on American manufacturers. Some not only refuse to die but even dominate their businesses worldwide. At the same time Ford struggles to keep up with Toyota, Caterpillar thrives in competition with another Japanese powerhouse, Komatsu. Though Zenith has been hurt in consumer electronics, Hewlett-Packard and Tektronix together profitably control 50% of the world's industrial test and measurement instrument market. American forklift truck producers may retreat under Japanese pressure, but two U.S. chemical companies—Du Pont and Dow—dramatically outperform their competitors.

How do these American producers hold and even increase profitability against international competitors? By forging integrated, global strategies to exploit their potential; and by having a long-term outlook, investing aggressively, and managing factories carefully.

The main reason is that today's international competition in many industries is very different from what it has been. To succeed, an international company may need to change from a multidomestic competitor, which allows individual subsidiaries to compete independently in different domestic markets, to a global organization, which pits its entire worldwide system of product and market position against the competition. (For a more complete discussion of this distinction, see the ruled insert.)

The global company—whatever its nationality—tries to control leverage points, from cross-national production scale economies to the foreign competitors' sources of cash flow. By taking unconventional action, such as lowering prices of an important product or in key markets, the company makes the competitor's response more expensive and

Authors' note: We acknowledge that this article is based in part on a paper coauthored by Eric Vogt.

1 For a more detailed look at globalization, see Michael E. Porter, *Competitive Strategy.*

difficult. Its main objective is to improve its own effectiveness while eroding that of its competitors.

Not all companies can or should forge a global strategy. While the rewards of competing globally are great, so are the risks. Major policy and operating changes are required. Competing globally demands a number of unconventional approaches to managing a multinational business to sometimes allow:

Major investment projects with zero or even negative ROI.

Financial performance targets that vary widely among foreign subsidiaries.

Product lines deliberately overdesigned or underpriced in some markets.

A view of country-by-country market positions as interdependent and not as independent elements of a worldwide portfolio to be increased or decreased depending on profitability.

Construction of production facilities in both high and low labor-cost countries.

Not all international businesses lend themselves to global competition. Many are multidomestic in nature and are likely to remain so, competing on a domestic-market-by-domestic-market basis. Typically these businesses have products that differ greatly among country markets and have high transportation costs, or their industries lack sufficient scale economies to yield the global competitors a significant competitive edge.

Before entering the global arena, you must first decide whether your company's industry has the right characteristics to favor a global competitor. A careful examination of the economies of the business will highlight its ripeness for global competition.[1] Simply put, the potential for global competition is greatest when significant benefits are gained from worldwide volume—in terms of either reduced unit costs or superior reputation or service—and are greater than the additional costs of serving that volume.

Identifying potential economies of scale requires considerable insight. Advantages to increased volume may come not only from larger production plants or runs but also from more efficient logistics networks or higher volume distribution networks. Worldwide volume is also particularly advantageous in supporting high levels of investment in research and development; many industries requiring high levels of R&D, such as pharmaceuticals or jet aircraft, are global. The level of transport or importing costs will also influence the business's tendency to become

global. Transport is a relatively small portion of highly traded optical goods, for example, while it is a barrier in trading steel reinforcing bars.

Many businesses will not be able to take the global step precisely because their industries lack these characteristics. Economies of scale may be too modest or R&D spending too closely tied to particular markets. Products may differ significantly across country boundaries, or the industry may emphasize distribution, installation, and other local activities. Lead times may be short, as in fashion-oriented businesses and in many service businesses, including printing. Also, transportation costs and government barriers to trade may be high, and distribution may be fragmented and hard to penetrate. Many consumer nondurable businesses or low-technology assembly companies fall into this category, as do many heavy raw-material processing industries and wholesaling and service businesses.

Our investigation into the strategies of successful global companies leads us to believe that a large group of international companies have global potential, even though they may not know it. Almost every industry that is now global—automobiles and TV sets, for example—was not at one time. A company must see the potential for changing competitive interaction in its favor to trigger a shift from multidomestic to global competition. And because there is no guarantee that the business can become global, the company must be willing to risk the heavy investment that global competition requires.

A company that recognizes its business as potentially global but not yet so must ask itself whether it can innovate effectively and must understand its impact on the competition to find the best answers to these three questions:

What kind of strategic innovation might trigger global competition?

Is it in the best position among all competitors to establish and defend the advantages of global strategy?

What kind of resources—over how long a period—will be required to establish the leading position?

The successful global competitor

If your industry profile fits the picture we've drawn, you can better judge your ability to make

	Caterpillar	Komatsu
Exhibit I **Financial comparison of Caterpillar and Komatsu**		
1980 estimated sales of construction equipment	$ 7.2 billion	$ 2.0 billion
1974-1979 averages:		
Return on capital employed	13.6 %	4.0 %
Debt/equity	0.4 times	2.1 times
Return on equity	19.1 %	12.2 %
Percent of earnings retained	69 %	65 %
Spare parts as percent of total revenue (estimated)	30 % to 35 %	15 % to 20 %
Cash flow available from operations	$ 681 million	$ 140 million

Source:
Financial statements.

these kinds of unconventional decisions by looking at the way three global companies have succeeded. These organizations (American, European, and Japanese) exemplify the global competitor. They all perceive competition as global and formulate strategy on an integrated, worldwide basis. Each has developed a strategic innovation to change the rules of the competitive game in its particular industry. The innovation acts as a lever to support the development of an integrated global system but demands a market position strong enough to implement it.

Finally, the three companies have executed their strategies more aggressively and effectively than their competitors. They have built barriers to competitive responses based on careful assessment of competitors' behavior. All three have the financial resources and commitment needed to compete unconventionally and the organizational structure to manage an integrated system.

We will take a careful look at each of these three and how they developed the strategic innovation that led, on the one hand, to the globalization of their industries and, on the other, to their own phenomenal success. The first company's innovation was in manufacturing; the second, in technology; and the third, in marketing.

The Caterpillar case: warring with Komatsu

Caterpillar Tractor Company turned large-scale construction equipment into a global business and achieved world leadership in that business even when faced with an able Japanese competitor. This accomplishment was difficult for a variety of reasons. For one thing, specifications of construction equipment varied widely across countries. Also, machines are expensive to transport, and field distribution—including user financing, spare parts inventories, and repair facilities—is demanding and best managed locally.

Navy Seabees who left their Caterpillar equipment in other countries following World War II planted the seeds of globalization. The company established independent dealerships to service these fleets, and this base of units provided a highly profitable flow of revenue from spare parts, which paid for inventorying new units. The Caterpillar dealers quickly became self-sustaining and to this day are larger, better financed, and do a more profitable parts business than their competitors. This global distribution system is one of Cat's two major barriers against competition.

The company used its worldwide production scale to create its other barrier. Two-thirds of the total product cost of construction equipment is in

| Exhibit II | Ericsson's technology lever: reduction of software cost through modular design |

	Representative systems	New modules required	Existing modules used
Year 1	Södertalje, Sweden	57	0
Year 2	Orleans, France	22	57
Year 3	Åbo, Finland	0	77

Source:
Boston Consulting Group, *A Framework for Swedish Industrial Policy* (Uberforlag, Stockholm, 1978).

heavy components – engines, axles, transmissions, and hydraulics – whose manufacturing costs are capital intensive and highly sensitive to economies of scale. Caterpillar turned its network of sales in different countries into a cost advantage by designing product lines that use identical components and by investing heavily in a few large-scale, state-of-the-art component manufacturing facilities to fill worldwide demand.

The company then augmented the centralized production with assembly plants in each of its major markets – Europe, Japan, Brazil, Australia, and so on. At these plants Cat added local product features, avoiding the high transportation cost of end products. Most important, Cat became a direct participant in local economies. The company achieved lower costs without sacrificing local product flexibility and became a friend rather than a threat to local governments. No single "world model" was forced on the customer, yet no competitor could match Caterpillar's production and distribution cost.

Not that they haven't tried. The most recent – and greatest – challenge to Caterpillar has come from Komatsu (see *Exhibit I* for a financial comparison). Japan's leading construction equipment producer forged its own global strategy based on exporting high-quality products from centralized facilities with labor and steel cost advantages. Over the last decade Komatsu has gained some 15% of the world construction-equipment market, with a significant share of sales in nearly every product line in competition with Cat.

Caterpillar has maintained its position against Komatsu and gained world share. The two companies increasingly dominate the market vis-à-vis their competitors, who compete on a domestic or regional basis. What makes Caterpillar's strategy so potent? The company has fostered the development of four characteristics essential to defending a leading world position against a determined competitor:

1 **A global strategy of its own.** Caterpillar's integrated global strategy yields a competitive advantage in cost and effectiveness. Komatsu simply plays catch-up ball rather than pulling ahead. Facing a competitor that has consciously devised a global strategy, Komatsu is in a much weaker position than were Japanese TV and automobile manufacturers when they took off.

2 **Willingness to invest in manufacturing.** Caterpillar's top management appears committed to the kind of flexible automated manufacturing systems that allow full exploitation of the economies of scale from its worldwide sales volume.

3 **Willingness to commit financial resources.** Caterpillar is the only Western company

that matches Komatsu in capital spending per employee; in fact, its overall capital spending is more than three times that of the Japanese company. Caterpillar does not divert resources into other businesses or dissipate the financial advantage against Komatsu by paying out excessive dividends. Because Komatsu's profitability is lower than Caterpillar's, it must exhaust debt capacity in trying to match Cat's high investment rates.

4   **Blocking position in the Japanese market.** In 1963, Caterpillar formed a joint venture in Japan with Komatsu's long-standing but weaker competitor, Mitsubishi. Operationally, the venture serves the Japanese market. Strategically, it acts as a check on the market share and cash flow of Komatsu. Japan accounts for less than 20% of the world market but yields over 80% of Komatsu's worldwide cash flow. The joint venture is number two in market position, serving to limit Komatsu's profits. Japanese tax records indicate that the Cat-Mitsubishi joint venture has earned only modest profits, but it is of great strategic value to Caterpillar.[2]

L.M. Ericsson: Can small be beautiful?

L.M. Ericsson of Sweden has become a successful global competitor by developing and exploiting a technological niche. Most major international telephone-equipment producers operated first in large, protected home markets that allowed the most efficient economies of scale. The additional profits helped underwrite R&D and provided good competitive leverage. Sweden's home market is relatively small, yet Ericsson translated the advent of electronic switching technology into a powerful global lever that befuddled competitors in its international market niche. In the electromechanical era of the 1960s, the telephone switching equipment business was hardly global. Switching systems combine hardware and software. In the electromechanical stage, 70% of total installed costs lay in hardware and 70% of hardware cost was direct labor, manufacturing overhead, and installation of the equipment.

Each country's telephone system was unique, economies of scale were low, and the wage rate was more important than the impact of volume on costs. In the late 1960s, major international companies (including Ericsson) responded by moving electro-switching production to LDCs not only to take advantage of cheaper labor but also to respond to the desire of government telephone companies to source locally.

Eventually, each parent company centrally sourced only the core software and critical components and competed on a domestic-market-by-domestic-market basis. For its part, Ericsson concentrated investment in developing countries without colonial ties to Europe and in smaller European markets that lacked national suppliers and that used the same switching systems as the Swedish market.

The telecommunications industry became global when, in the 1970s, electronic switching technology emerged, radically shifting cost structures and threatening the market position Ericsson had carved for itself. Software is now 60% of total cost; 55% of hardware cost is in sophisticated electronic components whose production is highly scale sensitive. The initial R&D investment required to develop a system has jumped to more than $100 million, which major international companies could have amortized more easily than Ericsson. In addition, the move to electronics promised to destroy the long-standing relationships Ericsson enjoyed with smaller government telephone companies. And it appeared that individual electronic switching systems would require a large fixed-cost software investment for each country, making the new technology too expensive for the smaller telephone systems, on which Ericsson thrived.

Ericsson knew that the electronic technology would eventually be adapted to small systems. In the meantime, it faced the possibility of losing its position in smaller markets because of its inability to meet the ante for the new global competition.

The company responded with a preemptive strategic innovation—a modular technology that introduced electronics to small telephone systems. The company developed a series of modular software packages that could be used in different combinations to meet the needs of diverse telephone systems at an acceptable cost. Moreover, each successive system required fewer new modules. As *Exhibit II* shows, the first system—Södertalje in Sweden—required all new modules, but by the third year, the Ābo system in Finland required none at all. Thus the company rapidly amortized development costs and enjoyed economies of scale that steepened as the number of software systems sold increased. As a result, Ericsson was able to compete globally in small systems.

Ericsson's growth is accelerating as small telephone systems convert to electronics. The company now enjoys an advantage in software cost and variety that continually reinforces itself. Through this technology Ericsson has raised a significant entry barrier against other companies in the small-system market.

---

2 For more on this subject,
see Craig M. Watson,
"Counter-Competition Abroad to
Protect Home Markets,"
HBR January-February 1982, p. 40.

Honda's marketing genius

Before Honda became a global company, two distinct motorcycle industries existed in the world. In Asia and other developing countries, large numbers of people rode small, simple motorcycles to work. In Europe and America, smaller numbers of people drove big, elaborate machines for play. Since the Asian motorcycle was popular as an inexpensive means of transportation, companies competed on the basis of price. In the West, manufacturers used styling and brand image to differentiate their products. No Western market exceeded 100,000 units; wide product lines and small volumes meant slight opportunities for economies of scale. Major motorcycle producers such as Harley-Davidson of the United States, BMW of West Germany, and Triumph and BSA of the United Kingdom traded internationally but in only modest volumes.

Honda made its industry global by convincing middle-class Americans that riding motorcycles could be fun. Because of the company's marketing innovations, Honda's annual growth rate was greater than 20% from the late 1950s to the late 1960s. The company then turned its attention to Europe, with a similar outcome. Honda invested for seven full years before sustaining profitability in Europe, financing this global effort with cash flows earned from a leading market position at home and in the United States.

Three crucial steps were decisive in Honda's achievement. First, Honda turned market preference around to the characteristics of its own products and away from those of American and European competitors. Honda targeted new consumers and used advertising, promotions, and trade shows to convince them that its motorbikes were inexpensive, reliable, and easy to use. A large investment in the distribution network – 2,000 dealerships, retail missionaries, generous warranty and service support, and quick spare-parts availability – backed up the marketing message.

Second, Honda sustained growth by enticing customers with the upper levels of its product line. Nearly half of new bike owners purchased larger, more expensive models within 12 months. Brand loyalty proved very high. Honda exploited these trends by expanding from its line of a few small motorcycles to one covering the full range of size and features by 1975. The result: self-sustaining growth in dollar volume and a model mix that allowed higher margins. The higher volume reduced marketing and distribution costs and improved the position of Honda and other Japanese producers who invaded the 750cc "super bike" portion of the market traditionally reserved for American and European companies. Here Honda beat the competition with a bike that was better engi-

What is a global industry?

The nature of international competition among multinationals has shifted in a number of industries. *Multinational* generally denotes a company with significant operations and market interests outside its home country. The universe of these companies is large and varied, encompassing different kinds of organizations operating in different types of industries. From a strategic point of view, however, there are two types of industries in which multinationals compete: *multidomestic* and *global*. They differ in their economics and requirements for success.

In *multidomestic* industries a company pursues separate strategies in each of its foreign markets while viewing the competitive challenge independently from market to market. Each overseas subsidiary is strategically independent, with essentially autonomous operations. The multinational headquarters will coordinate financial controls and marketing (including brand-name) policies worldwide and may centralize some R&D and component production. But strategy and operations are decentralized. Each subsidiary is a profit center and expected to contribute earnings and growth commensurate with market opportunity.

In a multidomestic industry, a company's management tries to operate effectively across a series of worldwide positions, with diverse product requirements, growth rates, competitive environments, and political risks. The company prefers that local managers do whatever is necessary to succeed in R&D, production, marketing, and distribution but holds them responsible for results. In short, the company competes with other multinationals and local competitors on a market-by-market basis. A large number of successful U.S. companies are in multidomestic industries, including Procter & Gamble in household products, Honeywell in controls, Alcoa in aluminum, and General Foods in branded foods.

A *global* industry, in contrast, pits one multinational's entire worldwide system of product and market positions against another's. Various country subsidiaries are highly interdependent in terms of operations and strategy. A country subsidiary may specialize in manufacturing only part of its product line, exchanging products with others in the system. Country profit targets vary, depending on individual impact on the cost position or effectiveness of the entire worldwide system – or on the subsidiary's position relative to a key global competitor. A company may set prices in one country to have an intended effect in another.

In a global business, management competes worldwide against a small number of other multinationals in the world market. Strategy is centralized, and various aspects of operations are decentralized or centralized as economics and effectiveness dictate. The company seeks to respond to particular local market needs, while avoiding a compromise of efficiency of the overall global system.

A large number of U.S. multinationals are in global industries. Among them, along with their principal competitors, are: Caterpillar and Komatsu in large construction equipment; Timex, Seiko, and Citizen in watches; General Electric, Siemens, and Mitsubishi in heavy electrical equipment.

The multidomestic and global labels apply to distinct industries and industry segments, not necessarily to whole industry groups. For example, within the electrical equipment industry, heavy apparatus such as steam turbine generators and large electric motors is typically global while low-voltage building controls and electrical fittings are multidomestic in nature.

neered, lower priced, and whose development cost was shared over the company's wide product line.

The third step Honda took was to exploit economies of scale through both centralized manufacturing and logistics. The increasing volume of engines and bike assemblies sold (50,000 units per month and up) enabled the company to use less costly manufacturing techniques unavailable to motorcycle producers with lower volumes (see *Exhibit III*). Over a decade, Honda's factory productivity rose at an average annual rate of 13.1% – several times higher than European and American producers. Combined with lower transportation cost, Honda's increased output gave it a landed cost per unit far lower than the competition's. In turn, the lower production cost helped fund Honda's heavy marketing and distribution investment. Finally, economies of scale in marketing and distribution, combined with low production cost, led to the high profits that financed Honda's move into automobiles.

What can we learn?

Each of these successful global players changed the dynamics of its industry and pulled away from its major competitors. By achieving economies of scale through commonality of design, Caterpillar exploited both its worldwide sales volume and its existing market for parts revenues. Competitors could not match its costs or profits and therefore could not make the investment necessary to catch up. Ericsson created a cost advantage by developing a unique modular technology perfectly adapted to its segment of the market. Its global strategy turned electronics from a threat to Ericsson into a barrier to its competitors. Honda used marketing to homogenize worldwide demand and unlock the potential for economies of scale in production, marketing, and distribution. The competition's only refuge was the highly brand-conscious, small-volume specialty market.

In each case, the industry had the potential for a worldwide system of products and markets that a company with a global strategy could exploit. Construction equipment offered large economies of scale in component manufacture, allowing Caterpillar to neutralize high transportation costs and government barriers through local assembly. Ericsson unlocked scale economies in software development for electronic switches. The modular technology accommodated local product differences and governments' desire to use local suppliers. Once Honda's marketing techniques raised demand in major markets for products with similar characteristics, the industry's economies of scale in production combined with low transportation costs and low tariff barriers to turn it into a global game.

In none of the cases did success result from a "world product." The companies accommodated local differences without sacrificing production costs. The global player's position in one major market strengthened its position in others. Caterpillar's design similarities and central component facilities allowed each market to contribute to its already favorable cost structure. Ericsson's shared modules led to falling costs each time a system was sold in a new country. Honda drew on scale economies from the centralized production of units sold in each market and used its U.S. marketing and distribution experience to succeed in Europe.

In addition to superior effectiveness and cost advantages, a winning global strategy always requires abilities in two other dimensions. The first is timing. The successful global competitor uses a production cost or distribution advantage as a leverage point to make it more difficult or expensive for the competitor to respond. The second is financial. The global innovator commits itself to major investment before anyone else, whether in technology, facilities, or distribution. If successful, it then reaps the benefits from increased cash flows from either higher volume (Honda and Ericsson) or lower costs (all three companies). The longer the competitor takes to respond, the larger the innovator's cash flows. The global company can then deploy funds either to increase investment or lower prices, creating barriers to new market entrants.

A global player should decide against which of its major competitors it must succeed first in order to generate broad-based success in the future. Caterpillar located in the Far East not only to source products locally but also to track Komatsu. (Cat increasingly sources product and manufacturing technology from Japan.) Ericsson's radical departure in technology was aimed squarely at ITT and Siemens, whose large original market shares would ordinarily have given them an advantage in the smaller European and African markets. Honda created new markets in the United States and Europe because its most powerful competitors, Yamaha and Kawasaki, were Japanese. By exploiting the global opportunity first, Honda got a head start, and it remained strong even when competitors' own international ambitions came to light.

Playing the global chess game

Global competition forces top management to change the way it thinks about and operates its businesses. Policies that made sense when the company was multidomestic may now be counterproduc-

| Exhibit III | The effect of volume on manufacturing approaches in motorcycle production |

Cost element	Low volume	High volume
Machine tools	Manual, general purpose	Numerical control, special purpose
Changeover time	Manual, slow (hours)	Automatic positioning, fast (minutes)
Work-in-process inventory	High (days of production)	Low (hours of production)
Materials handling	Forklift trucks	Automated
Assembly	Bay assembly	Motorized assembly line
Machine tool design	Designed outside the company, available throughout industry	Designed in-house, proprietary
Rework	More	Less

Source:
Strategy Alternatives for the British Motorcycle Industry,
a report prepared for the British Secretary of State for Industry
by the Boston Consulting Group, July 30, 1975.

| Exhibit IV | Honda Motor Company's financial policy from 1954 to 1980 |

Period	Interest-bearing debt-to-equity ratio	Strategic phase
1954-55	3.5 times	Rapid growth in domestic motorcycle market; Honda is low-margin, number two producer
1959-60	0.5	Domestic motorcycle market matured; Honda is dominant, high-margin producer
1964-65	0.7	Honda makes major penetration of U.S. motorcycle market
1969-70	1.6	Honda begins major move in domestic auto market
1974-75	1.3	Investment pause due to worldwide recession; motorcycle is major cash generator
1978-80	1.0	Auto exports are highly profitable, as are motorcycles

Source:
Annual reports.

tive. The most powerful moves are those that improve the company's worldwide cost position or ability to differentiate itself and weaken key worldwide competitors. Let us consider two potential moves.

The first is preempting the leading positions in major newly industrializing countries (NICs). Rapid growth in, for example, Mexico, Brazil, and Indonesia has made them an important part of the worldwide market for many capital goods. If its industry has the potential to become global, the company that takes a leading position in these markets will have made a decisive move to bar its competitors. Trade barriers are often prohibitively high in these places, and a company that tries to penetrate the market through a *self-contained* local subsidiary is likely to fall into a trap.

The astute global competitor will exploit the situation, however, by building a specialized component manufacturing facility in an NIC which will become an integral part of a global sourcing network. The company exports output of the specialized facility to offset importing complementary components. Final assembly for the domestic and smaller, neighboring markets can be done locally. (Having dual sources for key items can minimize the risk of disruption to the global sourcing network.)

A good illustration of this strategy is Siemens's circuit breaker operation in Brazil. When the company outgrew its West German capacity for some key components, it seized the opportunity presented by Brazilian authorities seeking capital investments in the heavy electrical equipment industry. Siemens now builds a large portion of its common components there, swaps them for other components made in Europe, and is the lowest-cost and leading supplier of finished product in Brazil.

Another move that can be decisive in a global industry is to establish a solid position with your largest customers to block competitors. Many businesses have a few customers that dominate the global market. The global competitor recognizes their importance and prevents current or prospective competitors from generating any sales.

A good example is a British company, BSR, the world's largest producer of automatic record changers. In the 1970s, when Japanese exports of audio equipment were growing rapidly, BSR recognized that it could lose its market base in the United States and Europe if the Japanese began marketing record changers. BSR redesigned its product to Japanese specifications and offered distributors aggressive price discounts and inventory support. The Japanese could not justify expanding their own capacity. BSR not only stalled the entry of the Japanese into the record-changer market but it also moved ahead of its existing competitor, Garrard.

A global company can apply similar principles to block the competition's access to key dis-

tributors or retailers. Many American companies have failed to seize this opportunity in their unwillingness to serve large, private-label customers (e.g., Sears, Roebuck) or by neglecting the less expensive end of their product line and effectively allowing competitors access to their distributors. Japanese manufacturers in particular could then establish a toehold in industries like TV sets and farm equipment.

The decision on prices for pivotal customers must not be made solely on considerations of ROI. Equally important in global competition is the impact of these prices on prospective entrants and the cost of failing to protect and expand the business base. One way to control the worldwide chess game in your favor is to differentiate prices among countries.

Manage interdependently

The successful global competitor manages its business in various countries as a single system, not a portfolio of independent positions. In the view of portfolio planning theory, a market's attractiveness and the strength of a company's position within it determine the extent of corporate resources devoted to it. A company should defend strong positions and try to turn weak ones around or abandon them. It will pursue high-profit and/or high-growth markets more aggressively than lower-profit or lower-growth ones, and it will decide on a stand-alone basis whether to compete in a market.

Accepting this portfolio view of international competition can be disastrous in a global industry. The global competitor focuses instead on its ability to leverage positions in one country market against those in other markets. In the global system, the ability to leverage is as important as market attractiveness; the company need not turn around weak positions for them to be useful.

The most obvious leverage a company obtains from a country market is the volume it contributes to the company's overall cost or effectiveness. Du Pont and Texas Instruments have patiently won a large sales volume in the sophisticated Japanese market, for example, which supports their efforts elsewhere. Winning a share of a market that consistently supports product innovation ahead of other markets—like the United States in long-haul jet aircraft—is another leverage point. The competitor with a high share of such a market can always justify new product investment. Or a market can contribute leverage if it supports an efficient scale manufacturing facility for a region—like Brazil for Siemens. Finally, a market can contribute leverage if a position in it can be used to affect a competitor's cash flow.

Organization: the Achilles heel

Organizational structure and reporting relationships present subtle problems for a global strategy. Effective strategic control argues for a central product-line organization; effective local responsiveness, for a geographic organization with local autonomy. A global strategy demands that the product-line organization have the *ultimate* authority, because without it the company cannot gain systemwide benefits. Nevertheless, the company still must balance product and area needs. In short, there is no simple solution. But there are some guidelines to help.

No one organization structure applies to all of a company's international businesses. It may be unnecessarily cumbersome, for example, to impose a matrix structure on all business. Organizational reporting lines should probably differ by country market depending on that market's role. An important market that offers high leverage, as in the foregoing examples, must work closely with the global business-unit managers at headquarters. Coordination is crucial to success. But the manager of a market outside the global system will require only sets of objectives under a regional reporting system.

Another guideline is that organizational reporting lines and structures should change as the nature of the international business changes. When a business becomes global, the emphasis should shift toward centralization. As countries increase in importance, they must be brought within the global manager's reach. Over time, if the business becomes less global, the company's organization may emphasize local autonomy.

The common tendency to apply one organizational structure to all operations is bound to be a disadvantage to some of them. In some U.S. companies, this approach inhibited development of the global strategy their industries required.

Match financial policies to competitive realities

If top management is not careful, adherence to conventional financial management and prac-

tices may constrain a good competitive response in global businesses. While capital budgeters use such standard financial tools as DCF return analysis or risk profiles to judge investments and creditors and stock analysts prefer stable debt and dividend policies, a global company must chart a different course.

Allocating capital

In a global strategy, investments are usually a long-term, interdependent series of capital commitments, which are not easily associated with returns or risks. The company has to be aware of the size and timing of the total expenditures because they will greatly influence competitors' new investment response. Most troublesome, however, is that revenues from investments in several countries may have to build up to a certain point before the company earns *any* return on investment.

A global strategy goes against the traditional tests for capital allocation: project-oriented DCF risk-return analysis and the country manager's record of credibility. Global competition requires a less mechanical approach to project evaluation. The successful global competitor develops at least two levels of financial control. One level is a profit and cost center for self-contained projects; the other is a strategy center for tracking interdependent efforts and competitors' performance and reactions. Global competitors operate with a short time frame when monitoring the execution of global strategy investments and a long time frame when evaluating such investments and their expected returns.

Debt & dividends

Debt and dividend policies should vary with the requirements of the integrated investment program of the whole company. In the initial stages, a company with a strong competitive position should retain earnings to build and defend its global position. When the industry has become global and growth slows or the returns exceed the reinvestment needed to retain position, the company should distribute earnings to the rest of the corporation and use debt capacity elsewhere, perhaps in funding another nascent global strategy.

Honda's use of debt over the last 25 years illustrates this logic (see *Exhibit IV*). In the mid-1950s, when Honda held a distant second place in a rapidly growing Japanese motorcycle industry, the company had to leverage its equity 3.5 times to finance growth. By 1960, the Japanese market had matured and

Honda emerged dominant. The debt-equity ratio receded to 0.5 times but rose again with the company's international expansion in motorcycles. In the late 1960s, Honda made a major move to the automobile market, requiring heavy debt. At that time, motorcycle cash flows funded the move.

Which strategic road to take?

There is no safe formula for success in international business. Industry structures continuously evolve. The Caterpillar, Ericsson, and Honda approaches will probably not work forever. Competitors will try to push industrial trends away from the strengths of the industry leaders, and technological or political changes may force the leading companies to operate in a multidomestic fashion once again.

Strategy is a powerful force in determining competitive outcomes, whether in international or domestic business. And although adopting a global strategy is risky, many companies can dramatically improve their positions by fundamentally changing the way they plan, control, and operate their businesses. But a global strategy requires that managers think in new ways. Otherwise the company will not be able to recognize the nature of competition, justify the required investments, or sustain the change in everyday behavior needed.

If the company can successfully execute a global strategy, it may find itself joining the ranks of the truly successful international companies. Whether they be Japanese, American, European, or otherwise, the strategic thread that ties together companies like IBM, Matsushita, K. Hattori (Seiko), Du Pont, and Michelin clearly shows that the rules of the international competitive game have changed. ▽

The merchant adventurer

Years ago, as a college professor, I used to walk downtown for lunch with a fellow intellectual. On the corner was a livery stable run by a man named Warren. As an adjunct to the livery business the old man conducted a hay and feed store. I can remember our satirical and superior comments on Mr. Warren's profession. "What a job, selling hay and feed! What interest can life hold for such a man?"

Later a bad physical breakdown forced me into outdoor work....So it was that in the space of ten years, by a process of involution, I had fetched a circuit and come round to the despised profession of Mr. Warren. And the curious thing was that I had come to like the hay and feed business and to find more real interest in it than in trying to teach college students something about Attila, the Hun, and Theodoric, the Ostrogoth.

If one's own little business teems with interest, the complex business of international trade fairly boils with it. Somebody has yet to write the epic of romance in business. The inventive genius, the passionate endeavor, the venturesome courage of the race are built into the unfolding drama of world trade....

We know something about the mighty influences which have shaped world trade in the past....Singularly enough, we understand less clearly what is going on in the world trade of our own day. If a man had the mental grasp and an amplified vision, he could write a five-pound book about the changes which are taking place beneath our eyes, changes of which we are only dimly and vaguely aware....

The charm of life is mystery. Mystery is romantic. The romance of world trade! That which lies ahead of the explorer, the merchant adventurer in all ages, the lure of the unknown, romance, mystery – mystery that ends in either peace and plenty or failure and defeat.

From
Alfred Pearce Dennis
The Romance of World Trade
(New York: Henry Holt and Company, 1926).

Reprint 82504

End-game strategies for declining industries

The strategy a company should follow in an industry's declining phase depends on its strengths relative to competitors' and how each views the prospects

Kathryn Rudie Harrigan and Michael E. Porter

During the last year or so you watched the demand for one of your business's products decline and noted that the same decline hit your competitors. Searching for a reason, you realize that your product may be becoming technologically obsolete. It looks as if it's just a question of time. Can you be profitable if you stay in and invest? What should your end-game strategy be?

Kathryn Harrigan and Michael Porter have studied the strategies of over 95 companies that confronted declining markets. They found that end games can sometimes be very profitable and that companies successful in end games ask themselves some crucial questions about the nature of the industry— what exit barriers face each competitor, how the pattern of decline will affect competition, and whether their relative strengths match the remaining pockets of

demand. The authors discuss the factors that determine the profitability of remaining in a declining industry as well as the strategic alternatives, and offer guidelines for choosing an end-game strategy.

Ms. Harrigan is assistant professor at the Columbia Business School. She has published numerous articles on strategic planning and is the author of Strategies for Declining Businesses *(D.C. Heath, 1980) and* Strategies for Vertical Integration *(D.C. Heath, 1983). Mr. Porter is professor at the Harvard Business School. He is the author of many articles and books on competition, including the well-known* Competitive Strategy: Techniques for Analyzing Industries and Competitors *(Free Press, 1980). His new book,* Advanced Competitive Strategy, *is due to appear in early 1984.*

Illustrations by Keith W. Jenkins.

End game *n* **1:** the last stage (as the last three tricks) in playing a bridge hand **2:** the final phase of a board game; specifically the stage of a chess game following serious reduction of forces.[1]

As early as 1948, when researchers discovered the "transistor effect," it was evident that vacuum tubes in television sets had become technologically obsolete. Within a few years, transistor manufacturers were predicting that by 1961 half the television sets then in use would employ transistors instead of vacuum tubes.

Since the 1950s, manufacturers of vacuum tubes have been engaged in the industry's end game. Like other end games, this one is played in an environment of declining product demand where conditions make it very unlikely that all the plant capacity and competitors put in place during the industry's heyday will ever be needed. In today's world of little or no economic growth and rapid technological change, more and more companies are being faced with the need to cope with an end game.

Because of its musical chair character, the end game can be brutal. Consider the bloodbath in U.S. gasoline marketing today. Between 1973 and 1983, in response to high crude oil prices and conservation efforts by consumers, the output from petroleum refineries declined precipitately. Uncertainty concerning

---

1 *Webster's Third New International Dictionary* (Springfield, Mass.: G.&C. Merriam, 1976).

The term has also been used for an existentialist play by Samuel Beckett.

supply and demand for refined products has made predicting the speed and extent of decline difficult, and an industry consensus has never evolved. Moreover, the competitors in this end game are very diverse in their outlooks and in the tactics they use to cope with the erratic nature of decline.

As in the baby food industry's end game, where a ten-year price war raged until demand plateaued, gasoline marketers and refiners are fighting to hold market shares of a shrinking pie. As industry capacity is painfully rationalized and companies dig in for the lean years ahead in their end game, a long period of low profits is inevitable.

In the vacuum tube industry, however, the end game was starkly different. Commercialization of solid-state devices progressed more slowly than the transistor manufacturers forecast. The last television set containing vacuum tubes was produced in 1974, and a vast population of electronic products requiring replacement tubes guaranteed a sizable market of relatively price-insensitive demand for some years. In 1983, several plants still produce tubes. Where obsolescence was a certainty and the decline rate slow, the six leading vacuum tube manufacturers were able to shut down excess plant capacity while keeping supply in line with demand. Price wars never ruined the profitability of their end game, and the companies that managed well during the decline earned satisfactorily high returns, particularly for declining businesses.

To recoup the maximum return on their investments, managers of some declining businesses are turning with considerable success to strategies that they had used only when demand was growing. In the past, the accepted prescription for a business on the wane has been a "harvest" strategy—eliminate investment, generate maximum cash flow, and eventually divest. The strategic portfolio models managers commonly use for planning yield this advice on declining industries: do not invest in low- or negative-growth markets; pull cash out instead.

Our study of declining industries suggests, however, that the nature of competition during a decline and the strategic alternatives available for coping with it are complex (see the accompanying insert for a description of the study). The experiences of industries that have suffered an absolute decline in unit sales over a sustained period differ markedly. Some industries, like vacuum receiving tubes, age gracefully, and profitability for remaining competitors has been extremely high. Others, like rayon, decline amid bitter warfare, prolonged excess capacity, and heavy operating losses.

The stories of companies that have successfully coped with decline vary just as widely. Some companies, like GTE Sylvania, reaped high returns by making heavy investments in a declining industry that made their businesses better sources of cash later. By selling out before their competitors generally recognized the decline, and not harvesting, other companies, like Raytheon and DuPont, avoided losses that competitors subsequently bore.

In this article we discuss the strategic problems that declining demand poses, where decline is a painful reality and not a function of the business cycle or other short-term discontinuities. Sometimes, of course, innovations, cost reductions, and shifts in other circumstances may reverse a decline.[2] Our focus here, however, is on industries in which available remedies have been exhausted and the strategic problem is coping with decline. When decline is beyond the control of incumbent companies, managers need to develop end-game strategies.

First, we sketch the structural conditions that determine if the environment of a declining industry is hospitable, particularly as these affect competition. Second, we discuss the generic end-game strategy alternatives available to companies in decline. We conclude with some principles for choosing an end-game strategy.

What determines the competition?

Shrinking industry sales make the decline phase volatile. The extent to which escalating competitive pressures erode profitability during decline, however, depends on how readily industry participants pull out and how fiercely the companies that remain try to contain their shrinking sales.

Conditions of demand

Demand in an industry declines for a number of reasons. Technological advances foster substitute products (electronic calculators for slide rules) often at lower cost or higher quality (synthetics for leather). Sometimes the customer group shrinks (baby foods) or buyers slide into trouble (railroads). Changes in life-style, buyers' needs, or tastes can also cause demand to decline (cigars and hatmaking equipment). Finally, the cost of inputs or complementary products may rise and shrink demand (recreational vehicles). The cause of decline helps determine how companies

---

2 See Michael E. Porter, *Competitive Strategy* (New York: Free Press, 1980), chapter 8.

The book also contains a treatment of exit barriers and other industry and competitor characteristics discussed in this article.

will perceive both future demand and the profitability of serving the diminished market.

Companies' expectations concerning demand will substantially affect the type of competitive environment that develops in an end game. The process by which demand in an industry declines and the characteristics of those market segments that remain also have a great influence on competition during the decline phase.

Uncertainty

Correct or not, competitors' perceptions of demand in a declining industry potently affect how they play out their end-game strategies. If managers in the industry believe that demand will revitalize or level off, they will probably try to hold onto their positions. As the baby food industry example shows, efforts to maintain position despite shrinking sales will probably lead to warfare. On the other hand, if, as was the case of synthetic sodium carbonate (soda ash), managers in different companies are all certain that industry demand will continue to decline, reduction of capacity is more likely to be orderly.

Companies may well differ in their perceptions of future demand, with those that foresee revitalization persevering. A company's perception of the likelihood of decline is influenced by its position in the industry and its difficulty in getting out. The stronger its stake or the higher its exit barriers, the more optimistic a company's forecast of demand is likely to be.

Rate & pattern of decline

Rapid and erratic decline greatly exacerbate the volatility of competition. How fast the industry collapses depends partly on the way in which companies withdraw capacity. In industrial businesses (such as the synthesis of soda ash) where the product is very important to customers but where a substitute is available, demand can fall drastically if one or two major producers decide to retire and customers doubt the continued availability of the original product. Announcements of early departure can give great impetus to the decline. Because shrinking volume raises costs and often prices, the decline rate tends to accelerate as time passes.

Structure of remaining demand pockets

In a shrinking market, the nature of the demand pockets that remain plays a major role in determining the remaining competitors' profitability. The remaining pocket in cigars has been premium-quality cigars, for example, while in vacuum tubes it has been replacement and military tubes.

If the remaining pocket has favorable structure, decline can be profitable for well-positioned competitors. For example, demand for premium-quality cigars is price insensitive: customers are immune to substitute products and very brand loyal. Thus, even as the industry declines, companies that offer branded, premium cigars are earning above-average returns. For the same reasons, upholstery leathers are a profitable market segment in the leather industry.

On the other hand, in the acetylene industry, ethylene has already replaced acetylene in some market segments and other substitutes threaten the remaining pockets. In those pockets, acetylene is a commodity product that, because of its high fixed manufacturing costs, is subject to price warfare. The potential for profit for its remaining manufacturers is dismal.

In general, if the buyers in the remaining demand pockets are price insensitive, e.g., buyers of replacement vacuum tubes for television receivers, or have little bargaining power, survivors can profit. Price insensitivity is important because shrinking sales imply that companies must raise prices to maintain profitability in the face of fixed overhead.

The profit potential of remaining demand pockets will also depend on whether companies that serve them have mobility barriers that protect them from attack by companies seeking to replace lost sales.

Exit barriers

Just as companies have to overcome barriers in entering a market, they meet exit barriers in leaving it. These barriers can be insurmountable even when a company is earning subnormal returns on its investment. The higher the exit barriers, the less hospitable the industry is during the industry's decline. A number of basic aspects of a business can become exit barriers.

Durable & specialized assets

If the assets, either fixed or working capital or both, are specialized to the business, company, or location in which they are being used, their diminished liquidation value creates exit barriers. A company with specialized assets such as sole-leather tanneries must either sell them to someone who intends to use them in the same business, usually in the same location, or scrap them. Naturally, few buyers wish to use the assets of a declining business.

Once the acetylene and rayon industries started to contract, for example, potential buyers for plants were few or nonexistent; companies sold plants at enormous discounts from book value to speculators or desperate employee groups. Particularly if it represents a large part of assets and normally turns over very slowly, specialized inventory may also be worth very little in these circumstances. The problem of specialized assets is more acute where a company must make an all-or-nothing exit decision (e.g., continuous process plants) versus a decision to reduce the number of sites or close down lines.

If the liquidation value of the assets is low, it is possible for a company to show a loss on the books but earn discounted cash flows that exceed the value that could be realized if management sold the business. When several companies perform this same analysis and choose to remain in a declining industry, excess capacity grows and profit margins are usually depressed.

By expanding their search for buyers, managers can lower exit barriers arising from specialized assets. Sometimes assets find a market overseas even though they have little value in the home country. But as the industry decline becomes increasingly clear, the value of specialized assets will usually diminish. For example, when Raytheon sold its vacuum tube-making assets in the early 1960s while tube demand was strong for color TV sets, it recovered a much higher liquidation than companies that tried to unload their vacuum tube facilities in the early 1970s, when the industry was clearly in its twilight years.

High costs of exit

Large fixed costs—labor settlements, contingent liabilities for land use, or costs of dismantling facilities—associated with leaving a business elevate exit barriers. Sometimes even after a company leaves, it will have to supply spare parts to past customers or resettle employees. A company may also have to break long-term contracts, which, if they can be abrogated at all, may involve severe cancellation penalties. In many cases, the company will have to pay the cost of having another company fulfill such contracts.

On the other hand, companies can sometimes avoid making fixed investments such as for pollution control equipment, alternative fuel systems, or maintenance expenditures by abandoning a business. These requirements promote getting out because they increase investment without raising profits, and improve prospects for decline.

Strategic considerations

A diversified company may decide to remain in a declining industry for strategic reasons even if the barriers just described are low. These reasons include:

Interrelatedness. A business may be part of a strategy that involves a group of businesses, such as whiskey and other distilled liquors, and dropping it would diminish overall corporate strategy. Or a business may be central to a company's identity or image, as in the case of General Cigar and Allied Leather, and leaving could hurt the company's relationships with key distribution channels and customers or lower the company's purchasing clout. Moreover, depending on the company's ability to transfer assets to new markets, quitting the industry may make shared plants or other assets idle.

Access to financial markets. Leaving an industry may reduce a company's financial credibility and lessen its attractiveness to acquisition candidates or buyers. If the divested business is large relative to the total, divestment may hurt earnings growth or in some way raise the cost of capital, even if the write-off is economically justified. The financial market is likely to ignore small operating losses over a period of years buried among other profitable businesses while it will react strongly to a single large loss. While a diversified company may be able to use the tax loss from a write-off to mitigate the negative cash flow impact of exit decisions, the write-off will typically still have an effect on financial markets. Recently the markets have looked favorably on companies who take their losses on businesses with little future, an encouraging sign.

Vertical integration. When companies are vertically integrated, barriers to exit will depend on whether the cause of decline touches the entire chain or just one link. In the case of acetylene, obsolescence made downstream chemical businesses, using acetylene as a feedstock, redundant; a company's decision whether to stay or go had to encompass the whole chain. In contrast, if a downstream unit depended on a feedstock that a substitute product had made obsolete, it would be strongly motivated to find an outside supplier of the substitute. In this case, the company's forward integration might hasten the decision to abandon the upstream unit because it had become a strategic liability to the whole company. In our study of endgame strategies, we found that most vertically integrated companies "deintegrated" before facing the final go/no go decision.

Information gaps

The more a business is related to others in the company, and especially when it shares assets or has a buyer-seller relationship, the more difficult it can be for management to get reliable information about its performance. For example, a failing coffee percolator unit may be part of a profit center with other small electrical housewares that sell well, and the company might not see the percolator unit's performance accurately and thus fail to consider abandoning the business.

Managerial resistance

Although the exit barriers we've described are based on rational calculations, or the inability to make them because of failures in informa-

Study of strategies for declining businesses

Compiling 20-year histories of industry competition and company departures, we studied the strategies of 61 companies in eight declining industries.* We interviewed key competitors in the rayon and acetate, cigar, baby food, electric percolator coffee maker, electronic vacuum receiving tube, acetylene, synthetic soda ash, and U.S. leather tanning industries. (Follow-up studies examined the petroleum refining and whiskey distilling industries and attained consistent results.) Leaving their industries, 42 companies were profitable or did not suffer significant losses, while 19 were unprofitable or suffered sizable losses. Thirty-nine of the 42 successful companies followed the prescriptions of the strategy matrix shown in *Exhibit II*. Sixteen of the 19 unsuccessful companies acted contrary to the recommendations of the strategy matrix. In short, if companies followed the matrix recommendations, their chances for success were better than 92%, while if they did not follow them, their chances of success were about 15%.

*See Kathryn Rudie Harrigan's
Strategies for Declining Businesses
(Lexington, Mass.: D.C. Heath, 1980).

tion, the difficulties of leaving a business extend well beyond the purely economic. Managers' emotional attachments and commitments to a business – coupled with pride in their accomplishments and fears about their own futures – create emotional exit barriers. In a single-business company, quitting the business costs managers their jobs and creates personal problems for them such as a blow to their pride, the stigma of having "given up," severance of an identification that may have been longstanding, and a signal of failure that reduces job mobility.

It is difficult for managers of a sick division in a diversified company to propose divestment, so the burden of deciding when to quit usually falls on top management. But loyalty can be strong even at that level, particularly if the sick division is part of the historical core of the company or was started or acquired by the current CEO. For example, General Mills's decision to divest its original business, flour, was an agonizing choice that took management many years to make. And the suggestion that Sunbeam stop producing electric percolator coffee makers and waffle irons met stiff resistance in the boardroom.

In some cases, even though unsatisfactory performance is chronic, managerial exit barriers can be so strong that divestments are not made until top management changes.[3] Divestments are probably the most unpalatable decisions managers have to make.[4]

Personal experience with abandoning businesses, however, can reduce managers' reluctance to get out of an industry. In an industry such as chemicals where technological failure and product substitution are common, in industries where product lives are historically short, or in high-technology companies where new businesses continually replace old ones, executives can become used to distancing themselves from emotional considerations and making sound divestment decisions.

Social barriers
Because government concern for jobs is high and the price of divestiture may be concessions from other businesses in the company or other prohibitive terms, closing down a business can often be next to impossible, especially in foreign countries. Divestiture often means putting people out of work, and managers understandably feel concern for their employees. Workers who have produced vacuum tubes for 30 years may have little understanding of solid-state manufacturing techniques. Divestiture can also mean crippling a local economy. In the depressed Canadian pulp industry, closing down mills means closing down whole towns.[5]

Asset disposition
The manner in which companies dispose of assets can strongly influence the profitability of a declining industry and create or destroy exit barriers for competitors. If a company doesn't retire a large plant but sells it to a group of entrepreneurs at a low price, the industry capacity does not change but the competition does. The new entity can make pricing decisions and take other actions that are rational for it but cripple the competition. Thus if the owners of a plant don't retire assets but sell out instead, the remaining competitors can suffer more than if the original owners had stayed on.

Volatility of end game

Because of falling sales and excess capacity, competitors fighting in an end game are likely to resort to fierce price warfare. Aggression is especially likely if the industry has maverick competitors with diverse goals and outlooks and high exit barriers, or if the market is very inhospitable (see *Exhibit I*).

As an industry declines, it can become less important to suppliers (which raises costs or diminishes service) while the power of distributors increases. In the cigar business, for example, because cigars are an impulse item, shelf positioning is crucial to success, and it's the distributor who deals with the retailer. In the whiskey trade too, distillers hotly compete for the best wholesalers. Decline has led to substantial price pressures from these powerful middlemen that have reduced profitability. On the other hand, if the industry is a key customer, suppliers may attempt to help fight off decline as, for example, pulp producers helped the rayon industry fight cotton.

Perhaps the worst kind of waning-industry environment occurs when one or more weakened companies with significant corporate resources are committed to stay in the business. Their weakness forces them to use desperate actions, such as cutting prices, and their staying power forces other companies to respond likewise.

Strategic alternatives for declining businesses

Discussions of strategy for shrinking industries usually focus on divestment or harvest strategies, but managers should consider two other alternatives as well – leadership and niche. These four strategies for decline vary greatly, not only in their goals but also in their implications for investment, and managers can pursue them individually or, in some cases, sequentially:

Exhibit I	**Structural factors that influence the attractiveness of declining industry environments**	

Structural factors	Environmental attractiveness	
	Hospitable	Inhospitable

Conditions of demand		
Speed of decline	Very slow	Rapid or erratic
Certainty of decline	100% certain predictable patterns	Great uncertainty, erratic patterns
Pockets of enduring demand	Several or major ones	No niches
Product differentiation	Brand loyalty	Commodity-like products
Price stability	Stable, price premiums attainable	Very unstable, pricing below costs

Exit barriers		
Reinvestment requirements	None	High, often mandatory and involving capital assets
Excess capacity	Little	Substantial
Asset age	Mostly old assets	Sizable new assets and old ones not retired
Resale markets for assets	Easy to convert or sell	No markets available, substantial costs to retire
Shared facilities	Few free-standing plants	Substantial and interconnected with important businesses
Vertical integration	Little	Substantial
"Single product" competitors	None	Several large companies

Rivalry determinants		
Customer industries	Fragmented, weak	Strong bargaining power
Customer switching costs	High	Minimal
Diseconomies of scale	None	Substantial penalty
Dissimilar strategic groups	Few	Several in same target markets

Leadership. A company following the market-share leadership strategy tries to reap above-average profitability by becoming one of the few companies remaining in a declining industry. Once a company attains this position, depending on the subsequent pattern of industry sales, it usually switches to a holding position or controlled harvest strategy. The underlying premise is that by achieving leadership the company can be more profitable (taking the investment into account) because it can exert more control over the process of decline and avoid destabilizing price competition. Investing in a slow or diminishing market is risky because capital may be frozen and resistant to retrieval through profits or liquidation. Under this strategy, however, the company's dominant position in the industry should give it cost leadership or differentiation that allows recovery of assets even if it reinvests during the decline period.

Managers can achieve a leadership position via several tactical maneuvers:

☐ Ensure that other companies rapidly retire from the industry. H.J. Heinz and Gerber Products took aggressive competitive actions in pricing, marketing, and other areas that built market share and dispelled competitors' dreams of battling it out.

☐ Reduce competitors' exit barriers. GTE Sylvania built market share by acquiring competitors' product lines at prices above the going rate. American Viscose purchased—and retired—competitors' capacity. (Taking this step ensures that others within the industry do not buy the capacity.) General Electric manufactured spare parts for competitors' products. Rohm & Haas took over competitors' long-term contracts in the acetylene industry. Proctor-Silex produced private-label goods for competitors so that they could stop their manufacturing operations.

☐ Develop and disclose credible market information. Reinforcing other managers' certainty about the inevitability of decline makes it less likely that competitors will overestimate the prospects for the industry and remain in it.

☐ Raise the stakes. Precipitating the need of other competitors to reinvest in new products or

3 See, for example, Stuart C. Gilmour, "The Divestment Decision Process," DBA dissertation, Harvard Graduate School of Business Administration, 1973; and Kathryn Rudie Harrigan, *Strategies for Declining Businesses* (Lexington, Mass.: D.C. Heath, 1980).

4 See Michael E. Porter, *Interbrand Choice, Strategy and Bilateral Market Power* (Cambridge: Harvard University Press, 1976).

5 See Nitin T. Mehta, "Policy Formulation in a Declining Industry: The Case of the Canadian Dissolving Pulp Industry," DBA dissertation, Harvard Graduate School of Business Administration, 1978.

process improvements makes it more costly for them to stay in the business.

Niche. The objective of this focus strategy is to identify a segment of the declining industry that will either maintain stable demand or decay slowly, and that has structural characteristics allowing high returns. A company then moves preemptively to gain a strong position in this segment while disinvesting from other segments. Armira followed a niche strategy in leather tanning, as Courtaulds did in rayon. To reduce either competitors' exit barriers from the chosen segment or their uncertainty about the segment's profitability, management might decide to take some of the actions listed under the leadership strategy.

Harvest. In the harvest strategy, undergoing a controlled disinvestment, management seeks to get the most cash flow it can from the business. DuPont followed this course with its rayon business and BASF Wyandotte did the same in soda ash. To increase cash flow, management eliminates or severely curtails new investment, cuts maintenance of facilities, and reduces advertising and research while reaping the benefits of past goodwill. Other common harvest tactics include reducing the number of models produced; cutting the number of distribution channels; eliminating small customers; and eroding service in terms of delivery time (and thus reducing inventory), speed of repair, or sales assistance.

Companies following a harvest strategy often have difficulty maintaining suppliers' and customers' confidence, however, and thus some businesses cannot be fully harvested. Moreover, harvesting tests managers' skills as administrators because it creates problems in retaining and motivating employees. These considerations make harvest a risky option and far from the universal cure-all that it is sometimes purported to be.

Ultimately, managers following a harvest strategy will sell or liquidate the business.

Quick divestment. Executives employing this strategy assume that the company can recover more of its investment from the business by selling it in the early stages of the decline, as Raytheon did, than by harvesting and selling it later or by following one of the other courses of action. The earlier the business is sold, the greater is potential buyers' uncertainty about a future slide in demand and thus the more likely that management will find buyers either at home or in foreign countries for the assets.

In some situations it may be desirable to divest the business before decline or, as DuPont did with its acetylene business, in the maturity phase. Once it's clear that the industry is waning, buyers for

the assets will be in a strong bargaining position. On the other hand, a company that sells early runs the risk that its forecast will prove incorrect, as did RCA's judgment of the future of vacuum tubes.

Divesting quickly will force the company to confront its own exit barriers, such as its customer relationships and corporate interdependencies. Planning for an early departure can help managers mitigate the effect of these factors to some extent, however. For example, a company can arrange for remaining competitors to sell its products if it is necessary to continue to supply replacements, as Westinghouse Electric did for vacuum tubes.

Choosing a strategy for decline

With an understanding of the characteristics that shape competition in a declining industry and the different strategies they might use, managers can now ask themselves what their position should be:

Can the structure of the industry support a hospitable, potentially profitable, decline phase (see *Exhibit I*)?

What are the exit barriers that each significant competitor faces? Who will exit quickly and who will remain?

Do your company's strengths fit the remaining pockets of demand?

What are your competitors' strengths in these pockets? How can their exit barriers be overcome?

In selecting a strategy, managers need to match the remaining opportunities in the industry with their companies' positions. The strengths and weaknesses that helped and hindered a company during the industry's development are not necessarily those that will count during the end game, where success will depend on the requirements to serve the pockets of demand that persist and the competition for this demand.

Exhibit II displays, albeit crudely, the strategic options open to a company in decline. When, because of low uncertainty, low exit barriers, and so forth, the industry structure is likely to go through an orderly decline phase, strong companies can either seek leadership or defend a niche, depending on the value to them of remaining market segments. When a

Exhibit II	Strategies for declining businesses	
	Has competitive strengths for remaining demand pockets	**Lacks competitive strengths for remaining demand pockets**
Favorable industry structure for decline	Leadership or niche	Harvest or divest quickly
Unfavorable industry structure for decline	Niche or harvest	Divest quickly

company has no outstanding strengths for the remaining segments, it should either harvest or divest early. The choice depends, of course, on the feasibility of harvesting and the opportunities for selling the business.

When high uncertainty, high exit barriers, or conditions leading to volatile end-game rivalry make the industry environment hostile, investing to achieve leadership is not likely to yield rewards. If the company has strengths in the market segments that will persist, it can try either shrinking into a protected niche, or harvesting, or both. Otherwise, it is well advised to get out as quickly as its exit barriers permit. If it tries to hang on, other companies with high exit barriers and greater strengths will probably attack its position.

This simple framework must be supplemented by a third dimension of this problem—that is to say, a company's strategic need to remain in the business. For example, cash flow requirements may skew a decision toward harvest or early sale even though other factors point to leadership, as interrelationships with other units may suggest a more aggressive stance than otherwise. To determine the correct strategy a company should assess its strategic needs vis-à-vis the business and modify its end-game strategy accordingly.

Usually it is advantageous to make an early commitment to one end-game strategy or another. For instance, if a company lets competitors know from the outset that it is bent on a leadership position, it may not only encourage other companies to quit the business but also gain more time to establish its leadership. However, sometimes companies may want to bide their time by harvesting until indecisive competitors make up their minds. Until the situation is clear, a company may want to make preparations to invest should the leader go, and have plans to harvest or divest immediately should the leader stay. In any case, however, successful companies should *choose* an end-game strategy rather than let one be chosen for them.

The best course, naturally, is anticipation of the decline. If a company can forecast industry conditions, it may be able to improve its end-game position by taking steps during the maturity phase (sometimes such moves cost little in strategic position at the time):

☐   Minimize investments or other actions that will raise exit barriers unless clearly beneficial to overall corporate strategy.

☐   Increase the flexibility of assets so that they can accept different raw materials or produce related products.

☐   Place strategic emphasis on market segments that can be expected to endure when the industry is in a state of decline.

☐   Create customer-switching costs in these segments.

Avoiding checkmate

Finding your company's position in *Exhibit II* requires a great deal of subtle analysis that is often shortchanged in the face of severe operating problems during decline. Many managers overlook the need to make strategy in decline consistent with industry structure because decline is viewed as somehow different. Our study of declining industries revealed other factors common to profitable players:

They recognize decline. With hindsight, it is all too easy to admonish companies for being overoptimistic about the prospects for their declining industries' revitalization. Nevertheless, some executives, such as those of U.S. oil refineries, fail to look objectively at the prospects of decline. Either their identification with an industry is too great or their perception of substitute products is too narrow. The presence of high exit barriers may also subtly affect how managers perceive their environment; because bad omens are so painful to recognize, people understandably look for good signs.

Our examination of many declining industries indicates that the companies that are most objective about managing the decline process are also participants in the substitute industry. They have a clearer perception concerning the prospects of the substitute product and the reality of decline.

They avoid wars of attrition. Warfare among competitors that have high exit barriers, such as the leather tanning companies, usually leads to disaster. Competitors are forced to respond vigorously to others' moves and cannot yield position without a big investment loss.

They don't harvest without definite strengths. Unless the industry's structure is very favorable during the decline phase, companies that try to harvest without definite strengths usually collapse. Once marketing or service deteriorates or a company raises its prices, customers quickly take their business elsewhere. In the process of harvesting, the resale value of the business may also dissipate. Because of the competitive and administrative risks of harvesting, managers need a clear justification to choose this strategy.

They view decline as a potential opportunity. Declining industries can sometimes be extraordinarily profitable for the well-positioned players, as GE and Raytheon have discovered in vacuum tubes. Companies that can view an industry's decline as an opportunity rather than just a problem, and make objective decisions, can reap handsome rewards. ▽

Reprint 83409

National
Competitive Advantage

The Competitive Advantage of Nations

by Michael E. Porter

National prosperity is created, not inherited. It does not grow out of a country's natural endowments, its labor pool, its interest rates, or its currency's value, as classical economics insists.

A nation's competitiveness depends on the capacity of its industry to innovate and upgrade. Companies gain advantage against the world's best competitors because of pressure and challenge. They benefit from having strong domestic rivals, aggressive home-based suppliers, and demanding local customers.

In a world of increasingly global competition, nations have become more, not less, important. As the basis of competition has shifted more and more to the creation and assimilation of knowledge, the role of the nation has grown. Competitive advantage is

Harvard Business School professor Michael E. Porter is the author of Competitive Strategy *(Free Press, 1980) and* Competitive Advantage *(Free Press, 1985) and will publish* The Competitive Advantage of Nations *(Free Press) in May 1990.*

DRAWINGS BY LESLIE CABARGA

created and sustained through a highly localized process. Differences in national values, culture, economic structures, institutions, and histories all contribute to competitive success. There are striking differences in the patterns of competitiveness in every country; no nation can or will be competitive in every or even most industries. Ultimately, nations succeed in particular industries because their home environment is the most forward-looking, dynamic, and challenging.

These conclusions, the product of a four-year study of the patterns of competitive success in ten leading trading nations, contradict the conventional wisdom that guides the thinking of many companies and national governments – and that is pervasive today in the United States. (For more about the study, see the insert "Patterns of National Competitive Success.") According to prevailing thinking, labor costs, interest rates, exchange rates, and economies of scale are the most potent determinants of competitiveness. In companies, the words of the day are merger, alliance, strategic partnerships, collaboration, and supranational globalization. Managers are pressing for more government support for particular industries. Among governments, there is a growing tendency to experiment with various policies intended to promote national competitiveness – from efforts to manage exchange rates to new measures to manage trade to policies to relax antitrust – which usually end up only undermining it. (See the insert "What is National Competitiveness?")

These approaches, now much in favor in both companies and governments, are flawed. They fundamentally misperceive the true sources of competitive advantage. Pursuing them, with all their short-term appeal, will virtually guarantee that the United States – or any other advanced nation – never achieves real and sustainable competitive advantage.

We need a new perspective and new tools – an approach to competitiveness that grows directly out of an analysis of internationally successful industries, without regard for traditional ideology or current intellectual fashion. We need to know, very simply, what works and why. Then we need to apply it.

How Companies Succeed in International Markets

Around the world, companies that have achieved international leadership employ strategies that differ from each other in every respect. But while every successful company will employ its own particular strategy, the underlying mode of operation – the char-

acter and trajectory of all successful companies – is fundamentally the same.

Companies achieve competitive advantage through acts of innovation. They approach innovation in its broadest sense, including both new technologies and new ways of doing things. They perceive a new basis for competing or find better means for competing in old ways. Innovation can be manifested in a new product design, a new production process, a new marketing approach, or a new way of conducting training. Much innovation is mundane and incremental, depending more on a cumulation of small insights and advances than on a single, major technological breakthrough. It often involves

> The lure of the huge U.S. defense market has diverted the attention of U.S. companies from global commercial markets.

ideas that are not even "new" – ideas that have been around, but never vigorously pursued. It always involves investments in skill and knowledge, as well as in physical assets and brand reputations.

Some innovations create competitive advantage by perceiving an entirely new market opportunity or by serving a market segment that others have ignored. When competitors are slow to respond, such innovation yields competitive advantage. For instance, in industries such as autos and home electronics, Japanese companies gained their initial advantage by emphasizing smaller, more compact, lower capacity models that foreign competitors disdained as less profitable, less important, and less attractive.

In international markets, innovations that yield competitive advantage anticipate both domestic and foreign needs. For example, as international concern for product safety has grown, Swedish companies like Volvo, Atlas Copco, and AGA have succeeded by anticipating the market opportunity in this area. On the other hand, innovations that respond to concerns or circumstances that are peculiar to the home market can actually retard international competitive success. The lure of the huge U.S. defense market, for instance, has diverted the attention of U.S. materials and machine-tool companies from attractive, global commercial markets.

Information plays a large role in the process of innovation and improvement – information that either is not available to competitors or that they do not seek. Sometimes it comes from simple investment in research and development or market research; more often, it comes from effort and from openness and from looking in the right place unencumbered by blinding assumptions or conventional wisdom.

This is why innovators are often outsiders from a different industry or a different country. Innovation may come from a new company, whose founder has a nontraditional background or was simply not appreciated in an older, established company. Or the capacity for innovation may come into an existing company through senior managers who are new to the particular industry and thus more able to perceive opportunities and more likely to pursue them. Or innovation may occur as a company diversifies, bringing new resources, skills, or perspectives to another industry. Or innovations may come from another nation with different circumstances or different ways of competing.

With few exceptions, innovation is the result of unusual effort. The company that successfully implements a new or better way of competing pursues its approach with dogged determination, often in the face of harsh criticism and tough obstacles. In fact, to succeed, innovation usually requires pressure, necessity, and even adversity: the fear of loss often proves more powerful than the hope of gain.

Once a company achieves competitive advantage through an innovation, it can sustain it only through relentless improvement. Almost any advantage can be imitated. Korean companies have already matched the ability of their Japanese rivals to mass-produce standard color televisions and VCRs; Brazil-

> Change is an unnatural act, particularly in successful companies; powerful forces are at work to avoid it at all costs.

ian companies have assembled technology and designs comparable to Italian competitors in casual leather footwear.

Competitors will eventually and inevitably overtake any company that stops improving and innovating. Sometimes early-mover advantages such as customer relationships, scale economies in existing technologies, or the loyalty of distribution channels are enough to permit a stagnant company to retain its entrenched position for years or even decades. But sooner or later, more dynamic rivals will find a way to innovate around these advantages or create a better or cheaper way of doing things. Italian appliance producers, which competed successfully on the basis of cost in selling midsize and compact appliances through large retail chains, rested too long on this initial advantage. By developing more differentiated products and creating strong brand franchises, German competitors have begun to gain ground.

Ultimately, the only way to sustain a competitive advantage is to *upgrade it* – to move to more sophisticated types. This is precisely what Japanese automakers have done. They initially penetrated foreign markets with small, inexpensive compact cars of adequate quality and competed on the basis of lower labor costs. Even while their labor-cost advantage persisted, however, the Japanese companies were upgrading. They invested aggressively to build large modern plants to reap economies of scale. Then they became innovators in process technology, pioneering just-in-time production and a host of other quality and productivity practices. These process improvements led to better product quality, better repair records, and better customer-satisfaction ratings than foreign competitors had. Most recently, Japanese automakers have advanced to the vanguard of product technology and are introducing new, premium brand names to compete with the world's most prestigious passenger cars.

The example of the Japanese automakers also illustrates two additional prerequisites for sustaining competitive advantage. First, a company must adopt a global approach to strategy. It must sell its product worldwide, under its own brand name, through international marketing channels that it controls. A truly global approach may even require the company to locate production or R&D facilities in other nations to take advantage of lower wage rates, to gain or improve market access, or to take advantage of foreign technology. Second, creating more sustainable advantages often means that a company must make its existing advantage obsolete – even while it is still an advantage. Japanese auto companies recognized this; either they would make their advantage obsolete, or a competitor would do it for them.

As this example suggests, innovation and change are inextricably tied together. But change is an unnatural act, particularly in successful companies; powerful forces are at work to avoid and defeat it. Past approaches become institutionalized in standard operating procedures and management controls. Training emphasizes the one correct way to do anything; the construction of specialized, dedicated facilities solidifies past practice into expensive brick and mortar; the existing strategy takes on an aura of invincibility and becomes rooted in the company culture.

Patterns of National Competitive Success

To investigate why nations gain competitive advantage in particular industries and the implications for company strategy and national economies, I conducted a four-year study of ten important trading nations: Denmark, Germany, Italy, Japan, Korea, Singapore, Sweden, Switzerland, the United Kingdom, and the United States. I was assisted by a team of more than 30 researchers, most of whom were natives of and based in the nation they studied. The researchers all used the same methodology.

Three nations–the United States, Japan, and Germany–are the world's leading industrial powers. The other nations represent a variety of population sizes, government policies toward industry, social philosophies, geographical sizes, and locations. Together, the ten nations accounted for fully 50% of total world exports in 1985, the base year for statistical analysis.

Most previous analyses of national competitiveness have focused on single nation or bilateral comparisons. By studying nations with widely varying characteristics and circumstances, this study sought to separate the fundamental forces underlying national competitive advantage from the idiosyncratic ones.

In each nation, the study consisted of two parts. The first identified all industries in which the nation's companies were internationally successful, using available statistical data, supplementary published sources, and field interviews. We defined a nation's industry as internationally successful if it *possessed competitive advantage relative to the best worldwide competitors.* Many measures of competitive advantage, such as reported profitability, can be misleading. We chose as the best indicators the presence of substantial and sustained exports to a wide array of other nations and/or significant outbound foreign investment based on skills and assets created in the home country. A nation was considered the home base for a company if it was either a locally owned, indigenous enterprise or managed autonomously although owned by a foreign company or investors. We then created a profile of all the industries in which each nation was internationally successful at three points in time: 1971, 1978, and 1985. The pattern of competitive industries in each economy was far from random: the task was to explain it and how it had changed over time. Of particular interest were the connections or relationships among the nation's competitive industries.

In the second part of the study, we examined the history of competition in particular industries to understand how competitive advantage was created. On the basis of national profiles, we selected over 100 indus-tries or industry groups for detailed study; we examined many more in less detail. We went back as far as necessary to understand how and why the industry began in the nation, how it grew, when and why companies from the nation developed international competitive advantage, and the process by which competitive advantage had been either sustained or lost. The resulting case histories fall short of the work of a good historian in their level of detail, but they do provide insight into the development of both the industry and the nation's economy.

We chose a sample of industries for each nation that represented the most important groups of competitive industries in the economy. The industries studied accounted for a large share of total exports in each nation: more than 20% of total exports in Japan, Germany, and Switzerland, for example, and more than 40% in South Korea. We studied some of the most famous and important international success stories–German high-performance autos and chemicals, Japanese semiconductors and VCRs, Swiss banking and pharmaceuticals, Italian footwear and textiles, U.S. commercial aircraft and motion pictures–and some relatively obscure but highly competitive industries–South Korean pianos, Italian ski boots, and British biscuits. We also added a few industries because they appeared to be paradoxes: Japanese home demand for Western-character typewriters is nearly nonexistent, for example, but Japan holds a strong export and foreign investment position in the industry. We avoided industries that were highly dependent on natural resources: such industries do not form the backbone of advanced economies, and the capacity to compete in them is more explicable using classical theory. We did, however, include a number of more technologically intensive, natural-resource-related industries such as newsprint and agricultural chemicals.

The sample of nations and industries offers a rich empirical foundation for developing and testing the new theory of how countries gain competitive advantage. The accompanying article concentrates on the determinants of competitive advantage in individual industries and also sketches out some of the study's overall implications for government policy and company strategy. A fuller treatment in my book, *The Competitive Advantage of Nations*, develops the theory and its implications in greater depth and provides many additional examples. It also contains detailed descriptions of the nations we studied and the future prospects for their economies.

–Michael E. Porter

Successful companies tend to develop a bias for predictability and stability; they work on defending what they have. Change is tempered by the fear that there is much to lose. The organization at all levels filters out information that would suggest new approaches, modifications, or departures from the norm. The internal environment operates like an immune system to isolate or expel "hostile" individuals who challenge current directions or established thinking. Innovation ceases; the company becomes stagnant; it is only a matter of time before aggressive competitors overtake it.

The Diamond of National Advantage

Why are certain companies based in certain nations capable of consistent innovation? Why do they ruthlessly pursue improvements, seeking an ever-more sophisticated source of competitive advantage? Why are they able to overcome the substantial barriers to change and innovation that so often accompany success?

The answer lies in four broad attributes of a nation, attributes that individually and as a system constitute the diamond of national advantage, the playing field that each nation establishes and operates for its industries. These attributes are:

1. *Factor Conditions.* The nation's position in factors of production, such as skilled labor or infrastructure, necessary to compete in a given industry.

2. *Demand Conditions.* The nature of home-market demand for the industry's product or service.

3. *Related and Supporting Industries.* The presence or absence in the nation of supplier industries and other related industries that are internationally competitive.

4. *Firm Strategy, Structure, and Rivalry.* The conditions in the nation governing how companies are created, organized, and managed, as well as the nature of domestic rivalry.

These determinants create the national environment in which companies are born and learn how to compete. (See the diagram "Determinants of Na-

tional Competitive Advantage.") Each point on the diamond—and the diamond as a system—affects essential ingredients for achieving international competitive success: the availability of resources and skills necessary for competitive advantage in an industry; the information that shapes the opportunities that companies perceive and the directions in which they deploy their resources and skills; the goals of the owners, managers, and individuals in companies; and most important, the pressures on companies to invest and innovate. (See the insert "How the Diamond Works: The Italian Ceramic Tile Industry.")

When a national environment permits and supports the most rapid accumulation of specialized assets and skills—sometimes simply because of greater effort and commitment—companies gain a competitive advantage. When a national environment affords better ongoing information and insight into product and process needs, companies gain a competitive advantage. Finally, when the national environment pressures companies to innovate and invest, companies both gain a competitive advantage and upgrade those advantages over time.

Factor Conditions. According to standard economic theory, factors of production—labor, land, natural resources, capital, infrastructure—will determine the flow of trade. A nation will export those goods that make most use of the factors with which

Determinants of National Competitive Advantage

Firm Strategy, Structure, and Rivalry

Factor Conditions

Demand Conditions

Related and Supporting Industries

it is relatively well endowed. This doctrine, whose origins date back to Adam Smith and David Ricardo and that is embedded in classical economics, is at best incomplete and at worst incorrect.

In the sophisticated industries that form the backbone of any advanced economy, a nation does not inherit but instead creates the most important factors of production—such as skilled human resources or a scientific base. Moreover, the stock of factors that a nation enjoys at a particular time is less important than the rate and efficiency with which it creates, upgrades, and deploys them in particular industries.

The most important factors of production are those that involve sustained and heavy investment and are specialized. Basic factors, such as a pool of labor or a local raw-material source, do not constitute an advantage in knowledge-intensive industries. Companies can access them easily through a global strategy or circumvent them through technology. Contrary to conventional wisdom, simply having a general work force that is high school or even college educated represents no competitive advantage in modern international competition. To support competitive advantage, a factor must be highly specialized to an industry's particular needs—a scientific institute specialized in optics, a pool of venture capital to fund software companies. These factors are more scarce, more difficult for foreign competitors to imitate—and they require sustained investment to create.

Nations succeed in industries where they are particularly good at factor creation. Competitive advantage results from the presence of world-class institutions that first create specialized factors and then continually work to upgrade them. Denmark has two hospitals that concentrate in studying and treating diabetes—and a world-leading export position in insulin. Holland has premier research institutes in the cultivation, packaging, and shipping of flowers, where it is the world's export leader.

What is not so obvious, however, is that selective disadvantages in the more basic factors can prod a company to innovate and upgrade—a disadvantage in a static model of competition can become an advantage in a dynamic one. When there is an ample supply of cheap raw materials or abundant labor, companies can simply rest on these advantages and often deploy them inefficiently. But when companies face a selective disadvantage, like high land costs, labor shortages, or the lack of local raw materials, they *must* innovate and upgrade to compete.

Implicit in the oft-repeated Japanese statement, "We are an island nation with no natural resources," is the understanding that these deficiencies have only served to spur Japan's competitive innovation. Just-in-time production, for example, economized on prohibitively expensive space. Italian steel producers in the Brescia area faced a similar set of disadvantages: high capital costs, high energy costs, and no local raw materials. Located in Northern Lombardy, these privately owned companies faced staggering logistics costs due to their distance from southern ports and the inefficiencies of the state-owned Italian transportation system. The result: they pioneered technologically advanced minimills that require only modest capital investment, use less energy, employ scrap metal as the feedstock, are efficient at small scale, and permit producers to locate close to sources of scrap and end-use customers. In other words, they converted factor disadvantages into competitive advantage.

Disadvantages can become advantages only under certain conditions. First, they must send companies proper signals about circumstances that will spread to other nations, thereby equipping them to innovate in advance of foreign rivals. Switzerland, the nation that experienced the first labor shortages after World War II, is a case in point. Swiss companies responded to the disadvantage by upgrading labor productivity and seeking higher value, more sustainable market segments. Companies in most other parts of the world, where there were still ample workers, focused their attention on other issues, which resulted in slower upgrading.

The second condition for transforming disadvantages into advantages is favorable circumstances elsewhere in the diamond–a consideration that ap-

Demanding buyers in the domestic market can pressure companies to innovate faster.

plies to almost all determinants. To innovate, companies must have access to people with appropriate skills and have home-demand conditions that send the right signals. They must also have active domestic rivals who create pressure to innovate. Another precondition is company goals that lead to sustained commitment to the industry. Without such a commitment and the presence of active rivalry, a company may take an easy way around a disadvantage rather than using it as a spur to innovation.

For example, U.S. consumer-electronics companies, faced with high relative labor costs, chose to leave the product and production process largely unchanged and move labor-intensive activities to Taiwan and other Asian countries. Instead of upgrading their sources of advantage, they settled for labor-cost parity. On the other hand, Japanese rivals, confronted with intense domestic competition and a mature home market, chose to eliminate labor through automation. This led to lower assembly costs, to products with fewer components and to improved quality and reliability. Soon Japanese companies were build-

ing assembly plants in the United States–the place U.S. companies had fled.

Demand Conditions. It might seem that the globalization of competition would diminish the importance of home demand. In practice, however, this is simply not the case. In fact, the composition and character of the home market usually has a disproportionate effect on how companies perceive, interpret, and respond to buyer needs. Nations gain competitive advantage in industries where the home demand gives their companies a clearer or earlier picture of emerging buyer needs, and where demanding buyers pressure companies to innovate faster and achieve more sophisticated competitive advantages than their foreign rivals. The size of home demand proves far less significant than the character of home demand.

Home-demand conditions help build competitive advantage when a particular industry segment is larger or more visible in the domestic market than in foreign markets. The larger market segments in a nation receive the most attention from the nation's companies; companies accord smaller or less desirable segments a lower priority. A good example is hydraulic excavators, which represent the most widely used type of construction equipment in the Japanese domestic market–but which comprise a far smaller proportion of the market in other advanced nations. This segment is one of the few where there are vigorous Japanese international competitors and where Caterpillar does not hold a substantial share of the world market.

More important than the mix of segments per se is the nature of domestic buyers. A nation's companies gain competitive advantage if domestic buyers are the world's most sophisticated and demanding buyers for the product or service. Sophisticated, demanding buyers provide a window into advanced customer needs; they pressure companies to meet high standards; they prod them to improve, to innovate, and to upgrade into more advanced segments. As with factor conditions, demand conditions provide advantages by forcing companies to respond to tough challenges.

Especially stringent needs arise because of local values and circumstances. For example, Japanese consumers, who live in small, tightly packed homes, must contend with hot, humid summers and high-cost electrical energy–a daunting combination of circumstances. In response, Japanese companies have pioneered compact, quiet air-conditioning units powered by energy-saving rotary compressors. In industry after industry, the tightly constrained requirements of the Japanese market have forced companies to innovate, yielding products that are *kei-haku-tan-*

sho – light, thin, short, small – and that are internationally accepted.

Local buyers can help a nation's companies gain advantage if their needs anticipate or even shape those of other nations – if their needs provide ongoing "early-warning indicators" of global market trends. Sometimes anticipatory needs emerge because a nation's political values foreshadow needs that will grow elsewhere. Sweden's long-standing concern for handicapped people has spawned an increasingly competitive industry focused on special needs. Denmark's environmentalism has led to success for companies in water-pollution control equipment and windmills.

More generally, a nation's companies can anticipate global trends if the nation's values are spreading – that is, if the country is exporting its values and tastes as well as its products. The international success of U.S. companies in fast food and credit cards, for example, reflects not only the American desire for convenience but also the spread of these tastes to the rest of the world. Nations export their values and tastes through media, through training foreigners, through political influence, and through the foreign activities of their citizens and companies.

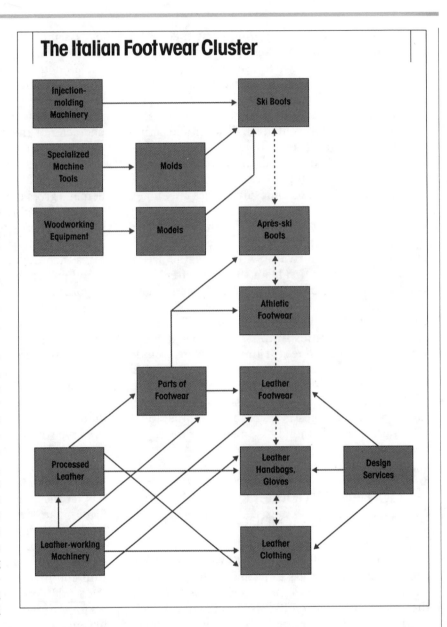

The Italian Footwear Cluster

Related and Supporting Industries. The third broad determinant of national advantage is the presence in the nation of related and supporting industries that are internationally competitive. Internationally competitive home-based suppliers create advantages in downstream industries in several ways. First, they deliver the most cost-effective inputs in an efficient, early, rapid, and sometimes preferential way. Italian gold and silver jewelry companies lead the world in that industry in part because other Italian companies supply two-thirds of the world's jewelry-making and precious-metal recycling machinery.

Far more significant than mere access to components and machinery, however, is the advantage that home-based related and supporting industries provide in innovation and upgrading – an advantage based on close working relationships. Suppliers and end-users located near each other can take advantage of short lines of communication, quick and constant flow of information, and an ongoing exchange of ideas and innovations. Companies have the opportunity to influence their suppliers' technical efforts and can serve as test sites for R&D work, accelerating the pace of innovation.

The illustration of "The Italian Footwear Cluster" offers a graphic example of how a group of close-by, supporting industries creates competitive advantage in a range of interconnected industries that are all internationally competitive. Shoe producers, for instance, interact regularly with leather manufacturers on new styles and manufacturing techniques and learn about new textures and colors of leather when they are still on the drawing boards. Leather manufacturers gain early insights into fashion trends, helping them to plan new products. The interaction is mutually advantageous and self-reinforcing, but it does not happen automatically: it is helped by proximity, but occurs only because companies and suppliers work at it.

The nation's companies benefit most when the suppliers are, themselves, global competitors. It is ultimately self-defeating for a company or country to create "captive" suppliers who are totally dependent on the domestic industry and prevented from serving foreign competitors. By the same token, a nation need not be competitive in all supplier industries for its companies to gain competitive advantage. Companies can readily source from abroad materials, components, or technologies without a major effect on innovation or performance of the industry's products. The same is true of other generalized technologies—like electronics or software—where the industry represents a narrow application area.

Home-based competitiveness in related industries provides similar benefits: information flow and technical interchange speed the rate of innovation and upgrading. A home-based related industry also increases the likelihood that companies will embrace new skills, and it also provides a source of entrants who will bring a novel approach to competing. The Swiss success in pharmaceuticals emerged out of previous international success in the dye industry, for example; Japanese dominance in electronic musical keyboards grows out of success in acoustic instruments combined with a strong position in consumer electronics.

Firm Strategy, Structure, and Rivalry. National circumstances and context create strong tendencies in how companies are created, organized, and managed, as well as what the nature of domestic rivalry will be. In Italy, for example, successful international competitors are often small or medium-sized companies that are privately owned and operated like extended families; in Germany, in contrast, companies tend to be strictly hierarchical in organization and management practices, and top managers usually have technical backgrounds.

No one managerial system is universally appropriate—notwithstanding the current fascination with Japanese management. Competitiveness in a specific industry results from convergence of the management practices and organizational modes favored in the country and the sources of competitive advantage in the industry. In industries where Italian companies are world leaders—such as lighting, furniture, footwear, woolen fabrics, and packaging machines—a company strategy that emphasizes focus, customized products, niche marketing, rapid change, and breathtaking flexibility fits both the dy-

namics of the industry and the character of the Italian management system. The German management system, in contrast, works well in technical or engineering-oriented industries—optics, chemicals, complicated machinery—where complex products demand precision manufacturing, a careful development process, after-sale service, and thus a highly disciplined management structure. German success is much rarer in consumer goods and services where image marketing and rapid new-feature and model turnover are important to competition.

Countries also differ markedly in the goals that companies and individuals seek to achieve. Company goals reflect the characteristics of national capital markets and the compensation practices for managers. For example, in Germany and Switzerland, where banks comprise a substantial part of the nation's shareholders, most shares are held for long-

> ## No one managerial system is universally appropriate—notwithstanding the current fascination with Japanese management.

term appreciation and are rarely traded. Companies do well in mature industries, where ongoing investment in R&D and new facilities is essential but returns may be only moderate. The United States is at the opposite extreme, with a large pool of risk capital but widespread trading of public companies and a strong emphasis by investors on quarterly and annual share-price appreciation. Management compensation is heavily based on annual bonuses tied to individual results. America does well in relatively new industries, like software and biotechnology, or ones where equity funding of new companies feeds active domestic rivalry, like specialty electronics and services. Strong pressures leading to underinvestment, however, plague more mature industries.

Individual motivation to work and expand skills is also important to competitive advantage. Outstanding talent is a scarce resource in any nation. A nation's success largely depends on the types of education its talented people choose, where they choose to work, and their commitment and effort. The goals a nation's institutions and values set for individuals and companies, and the prestige it attaches to certain industries, guide the flow of capital and human resources—which, in turn, directly affects the competitive performance of certain industries. Nations tend to be competitive in activities that people admire or depend on – the activities from which the nation's heroes emerge. In Switzerland, it is banking and pharmaceuticals. In Israel, the highest callings have been agriculture and defense-related fields. Sometimes it is hard to distinguish between cause and effect. Attaining international success can make an industry prestigious, reinforcing its advantage.

The presence of strong local rivals is a final, and powerful, stimulus to the creation and persistence of competitive advantage. This is true of small countries, like Switzerland, where the rivalry among its pharmaceutical companies, Hoffmann-La Roche, Ciba-Geigy, and Sandoz, contributes to a leading worldwide position. It is true in the United States in the computer and software industries. Nowhere is the role of fierce rivalry more apparent than in Japan, where there are 112 companies competing in machine tools, 34 in semiconductors, 25 in audio equipment, 15 in cameras – in fact, there are usually double figures in the industries in which Japan boasts global dominance. (See the table "Estimated Number of Japanese Rivals in Selected Industries.") Among all the points on the diamond, domestic rivalry is argu-

> **Local rivalries go beyond economic competition – they become intensely personal feuds for "bragging rights."**

ably the most important because of the powerfully stimulating effect it has on all the others.

Conventional wisdom argues that domestic competition is wasteful: it leads to duplication of effort and prevents companies from achieving economies of scale. The "right solution" is to embrace one or two national champions, companies with the scale and strength to tackle foreign competitors, and to guarantee them the necessary resources, with the government's blessing. In fact, however, most national champions are uncompetitive, although heavily subsidized and protected by their government. In many of the prominent industries in which there is only one national rival, such as aerospace and telecommunications, government has played a large role in distorting competition.

Static efficiency is much less important than dynamic improvement, which domestic rivalry uniquely spurs. Domestic rivalry, like any rivalry, creates pressure on companies to innovate and improve. Local rivals push each other to lower costs, improve quality and service, and create new products and processes. But unlike rivalries with foreign competitors, which tend to be analytical and distant,

Estimated Number of Japanese Rivals in Selected Industries

Air conditioners	13
Audio Equipment	25
Automobiles	9
Cameras	15
Car Audio	12
Carbon Fibers	7
Construction Equipment*	15
Copiers	14
Facsimile Machines	10
Large-scale Computers	6
Lift Trucks	8
Machine Tools	112
Microwave Equipment	5
Motorcycles	4
Musical Instruments	4
Personal Computers	16
Semiconductors	34
Sewing Machines	20
Shipbuilding†	33
Steel‡	5
Synthetic Fibers	8
Television Sets	15
Truck and Bus Tires	5
Trucks	11
Typewriters	14
Videocassette Recorders	10

Sources: Field interviews; *Nippon Kogyo Shinbun, Nippon Kogyo Nenkan,* 1987; Yano Research, *Market Share Jitan,* 1987; researchers' estimates.

*The number of companies varied by product area. The smallest number, 10, produced bulldozers. Fifteen companies produced shovel trucks, truck cranes, and asphalt-paving equipment. There were 20 companies in hydraulic excavators, a product area where Japan was particularly strong.
†Six companies had annual production exports in excess of 10,000 tons.
‡Integrated companies.

local rivalries often go beyond pure economic or business competition and become intensely personal. Domestic rivals engage in active feuds; they compete not only for market share but also for people, for technical excellence, and perhaps most important, for "bragging rights." One domestic rival's success proves to others that advancement is possible and often attracts new rivals to the industry. Companies often attribute the success of foreign rivals to "unfair" advantages. With domestic rivals, there are no excuses.

Geographic concentration magnifies the power of domestic rivalry. This pattern is strikingly common around the world: Italian jewelry companies are located around two towns, Arezzo and Valenza Po; cutlery companies in Solingen, West Germany and Seki, Japan; pharmaceutical companies in Basel, Switzerland; motorcycles and musical instruments in Hamamatsu, Japan. The more localized the rivalry, the more intense. And the more intense, the better.

Another benefit of domestic rivalry is the pressure it creates for constant upgrading of the sources of competitive advantage. The presence of domestic competitors automatically cancels the types of advantage that come from simply being in a particular nation—factor costs, access to or preference in the home market, or costs to foreign competitors who import into the market. Companies are forced to move beyond them, and as a result, gain more sustainable advantages. Moreover, competing domestic rivals will keep each other honest in obtaining government support. Companies are less likely to get hooked on the narcotic of government contracts or creeping industry protectionism. Instead, the industry will seek—and benefit from—more constructive forms of government support, such as assistance in opening foreign markets, as well as investments in focused educational institutions or other specialized factors.

Ironically, it is also vigorous domestic competition that ultimately pressures domestic companies to look at global markets and toughens them to succeed in them. Particularly when there are economies of scale, local competitors force each other to look outward to foreign markets to capture greater efficiency and higher profitability. And having been tested by fierce domestic competition, the stronger companies are well equipped to win abroad. If Digital Equipment can hold its own against IBM, Data General, Prime, and Hewlett-Packard, going up against Siemens or Machines Bull does not seem so daunting a prospect.

The Diamond as a System

Each of these four attributes defines a point on the diamond of national advantage; the effect of one point often depends on the state of others. Sophisticated buyers will not translate into advanced products, for example, unless the quality of human resources permits companies to meet buyer needs. Selective disadvantages in factors of production will not motivate innovation unless rivalry is vigorous and company goals support sustained investment. At the broadest level, weaknesses in any one determinant will constrain an industry's potential for advancement and upgrading.

But the points of the diamond are also self-reinforcing: they constitute a system. Two elements, domestic rivalry and geographic concentration, have especially great power to transform the diamond into a system—domestic rivalry because it promotes improvement in all the other determinants and geographic concentration because it elevates and magnifies the interaction of the four separate influences.

The role of domestic rivalry illustrates how the diamond operates as a self-reinforcing system. Vigorous domestic rivalry stimulates the development of unique pools of specialized factors, particularly if the

> ## Nations are rarely home to just one competitive industry; the diamond promotes industry *clusters*.

rivals are all located in one city or region: the University of California at Davis has become the world's leading center of wine-making research, working closely with the California wine industry. Active local rivals also upgrade domestic demand in an industry. In furniture and shoes, for example, Italian consumers have learned to expect more and better products because of the rapid pace of new product development that is driven by intense domestic rivalry among hundreds of Italian companies. Domestic rivalry also promotes the formation of related and supporting industries. Japan's world-leading group of semiconductor producers, for instance, has spawned world-leading Japanese semiconductor-equipment manufacturers.

The effects can work in all directions: sometimes world-class suppliers become new entrants in the industry they have been supplying. Or highly sophisticated buyers may themselves enter a supplier industry, particularly when they have relevant skills and view the new industry as strategic. In the case of the Japanese robotics industry, for example, Matsushita and Kawasaki originally designed robots for internal use before beginning to sell robots to others. Today they are strong competitors in the robotics industry. In Sweden, Sandvik moved from specialty steel into rock drills, and SKF moved from specialty steel into ball bearings.

Another effect of the diamond's systemic nature is that nations are rarely home to just one competitive industry; rather, the diamond creates an environment that promotes *clusters* of competitive industries. Competitive industries are not scattered helter-skelter throughout the economy but are usually linked together through vertical (buyer-seller) or horizontal (common customers, technology, channels) relationships. Nor are clusters usually scattered physically; they tend to be concentrated geographically. One competitive industry helps to create an-

What Is National Competitiveness?

National competitiveness has become one of the central preoccupations of government and industry in every nation. Yet for all the discussion, debate, and writing on the topic, there is still no persuasive theory to explain national competitiveness. What is more, there is not even an accepted definition of the term "competitiveness" as applied to a nation. While the notion of a competitive company is clear, the notion of a competitive nation is not.

Some see national competitiveness as a macroeconomic phenomenon, driven by variables such as exchange rates, interest rates, and government deficits. But Japan, Italy, and South Korea have all enjoyed rapidly rising living standards despite budget deficits; Germany and Switzerland despite appreciating currencies; and Italy and Korea despite high interest rates.

Others argue that competitiveness is a function of cheap and abundant labor. But Germany, Switzerland, and Sweden have all prospered even with high wages and labor shortages. Besides, shouldn't a nation seek higher wages for its workers as a goal of competitiveness?

Another view connects competitiveness with bountiful natural resources. But how, then, can one explain the success of Germany, Japan, Switzerland, Italy, and South Korea—countries with limited natural resources?

More recently, the argument has gained favor that competitiveness is driven by government policy: targeting, protection, import promotion, and subsidies have propelled Japanese and South Korean auto, steel, shipbuilding, and semiconductor industries into global preeminence. But a closer look reveals a spotty record. In Italy, government intervention has been ineffectual—but Italy has experienced a boom in world export share second only to Japan. In Germany, direct government intervention in exporting industries is rare. And even in Japan and South Korea, government's role in such important industries as facsimile machines, copiers, robotics, and advanced materials has been modest; some of the most frequently cited examples, such as sewing machines, steel, and shipbuilding, are now quite dated.

A final popular explanation for national competitiveness is differences in management practices, including management-labor relations. The problem here, however, is that different industries require different approaches to management. The successful management practices governing small, private, and loosely organized Italian family companies in footwear, textiles, and jewelry, for example, would produce a management disaster if applied to German chemical or auto companies, Swiss pharmaceutical makers, or American aircraft producers. Nor is it possible to generalize about management-labor relations. Despite the commonly held view that powerful unions undermine competitive advantage, unions are strong in Germany and Sweden—and both countries boast internationally preeminent companies.

Clearly, none of these explanations is fully satisfactory; none is sufficient by itself to rationalize the competitive position of industries within a national border. Each contains some truth; but a broader, more complex set of forces seems to be at work.

The lack of a clear explanation signals an even more fundamental question. What is a "competitive" nation in the first place? Is a "competitive" nation one where every company or industry is competitive? No nation meets this test. Even Japan has large sectors of its economy that fall far behind the world's best competitors.

Is a "competitive" nation one whose exchange rate makes its goods price competitive in international markets? Both Germany and Japan have enjoyed remarkable gains in their standards of living—and experienced sustained periods of strong currency and rising prices. Is a "competitive" nation one with a large positive balance of trade? Switzerland has roughly balanced trade; Italy has a chronic trade deficit—both nations enjoy strongly rising national income. Is a "competitive" nation one with low labor costs? India and Mexico both have low wages and low labor costs—but neither seems an attractive industrial model.

The only meaningful concept of competitiveness at the national level is *productivity*. The principal goal of a nation is to produce a high and rising standard of living for its citizens. The ability to do so depends on the productivity with which a nation's labor and capital are employed. Productivity is the value of the output produced by a unit of labor or capital. Productivity depends on both the quality and features of products (which determine the prices that they can command) and the efficiency with which they are produced. Productivity is the prime determinant of a nation's long-run standard of living; it is the root cause of national per capita income. The productivity of human resources determines employee wages; the productivity with which capital is employed determines the return it earns for its holders.

A nation's standard of living depends on the capacity of its companies to achieve high levels of productivity—and to increase productivity over time. Sustained productivity growth requires that an economy continually *upgrade itself*. A nation's companies must relentlessly improve productivity in existing industries by raising product quality, adding desirable features, improving product technology, or boosting production efficiency. They must develop the necessary capabilities to compete in more and more sophisticated industry segments, where productivity is generally high. They must finally develop the capability to compete in entirely new, sophisticated industries.

International trade and foreign investment can both improve a nation's productivity as well as threaten it. They support rising national productivity by allowing a nation to specialize in those industries and segments of industries where its companies are more productive and to import where its companies are less productive. No nation can be competitive in everything. The ideal is to deploy the nation's limited pool of human and other resources into the most productive uses. Even those nations with the highest standards of living have many industries in which local companies are uncompetitive.

Yet international trade and foreign investment also can threaten productivity growth. They expose a nation's industries to the test of international standards of productivity. An industry will lose out if its productivity is not sufficiently higher than foreign rivals' to offset any advantages in local wage rates. If a nation loses the ability to compete in a range of high-productivity/high-wage industries, its standard of living is threatened.

Defining national competitiveness as achieving a trade surplus or balanced trade per se is inappropriate. The expansion of exports because of low wages and a weak currency, at the same time that the nation imports sophisticated goods that its companies cannot produce competitively, may bring trade into balance or surplus but lowers the nation's standard of living. Competitiveness also does not mean jobs. It's the *type* of jobs, not just the ability to employ citizens at low wages, that is decisive for economic prosperity.

Seeking to explain "competitiveness" at the national level, then, is to answer the wrong question. What we must understand instead is the determinants of productivity and the rate of productivity growth. To find answers, we must focus not on the economy as a whole but on *specific industries and industry segments*. We must understand how and why commercially viable skills and technology are created, which can only be fully understood at the level of particular industries. It is the outcome of the thousands of struggles for competitive advantage against foreign rivals in particular segments and industries, in which products and processes are created and improved, that underpins the process of upgrading national productivity.

When one looks closely at any national economy, there are striking differences among a nation's industries in competitive success. International advantage is often concentrated in particular industry segments. German exports of cars are heavily skewed toward high-performance cars, while Korean exports are all compacts and subcompacts. In many industries and segments of industries, the competitors with true international competitive advantage are *based in only a few nations*.

Our search, then, is for the decisive characteristic of a nation that allows its companies to create and sustain competitive advantage in particular fields – the search is for the competitive advantage of nations. We are particularly concerned with the determinants of international success in technology- and skill-intensive segments and industries, which underpin high and rising productivity.

Classical theory explains the success of nations in particular industries based on so-called factors of production such as land, labor, and natural resources. Nations gain factor-based comparative advantage in industries that make intensive use of the factors they possess in abundance. Classical theory, however, has been overshadowed in advanced industries and economies by the globalization of competition and the power of technology.

A new theory must recognize that in modern international competition, companies compete with global strategies involving not only trade but also foreign investment. What a new theory must explain is why a nation provides a favorable *home base* for companies that compete internationally. The home base is the nation in which the essential competitive advantages of the enterprise are created and sustained. It is where a company's strategy is set, where the core product and process technology is created and maintained, and where the most productive jobs and most advanced skills are located. The presence of the home base in a nation has the greatest positive influence on other linked domestic industries and leads to other benefits in the nation's economy. While the ownership of the company is often concentrated at the home base, the nationality of shareholders is secondary.

A new theory must move beyond comparative advantage to the competitive advantage of a nation. It must reflect a rich conception of competition that includes segmented markets, differentiated products, technology differences, and economies of scale. A new theory must go beyond cost and explain why companies from some nations are better than others at creating advantages based on quality, features, and new product innovation. A new theory must begin from the premise that competition is dynamic and evolving; it must answer the questions: Why do some companies based in some nations innovate more than others? Why do some nations provide an environment that enables companies to improve and innovate faster than foreign rivals?
                                                              —Michael E. Porter

other in a mutually reinforcing process. Japan's strength in consumer electronics, for example, drove its success in semiconductors toward the memory chips and integrated circuits these products use. Japanese strength in laptop computers, which contrasts to limited success in other segments, reflects the base of strength in other compact, portable products and leading expertise in liquid-crystal display gained in the calculator and watch industries.

Once a cluster forms, the whole group of industries becomes mutually supporting. Benefits flow forward, backward, and horizontally. Aggressive rivalry in one industry spreads to others in the cluster, through spin-offs, through the exercise of bargaining power, and through diversification by established companies. Entry from other industries within the cluster spurs upgrading by stimulating diversity in R&D approaches and facilitating the introduction of new strategies and skills. Through the conduits of suppliers or customers who have contact with multiple competitors, information flows freely and innovations diffuse rapidly. Interconnections within the cluster, often unanticipated, lead to perceptions of new ways of competing and new opportunities. The cluster becomes a vehicle for maintaining diversity and overcoming the inward focus, inertia, inflexibility, and accommodation among rivals that slows or blocks competitive upgrading and new entry.

The Role of Government

In the continuing debate over the competitiveness of nations, no topic engenders more argument or creates less understanding than the role of the government. Many see government as an essential helper or supporter of industry, employing a host of policies to contribute directly to the competitive performance of strategic or target industries. Others accept the "free market" view that the operation of the economy should be left to the workings of the invisible hand.

Both views are incorrect. Either, followed to its logical outcome, would lead to the permanent erosion of a country's competitive capabilities. On one hand, advocates of government help for industry frequently propose policies that would actually hurt companies in the long run and only create the demand for more helping. On the other hand, advocates of a diminished government presence ignore the legitimate role that government plays in shaping the context and institutional structure surrounding companies and in creating an environment that stimulates companies to gain competitive advantage.

Government's proper role is as a catalyst and challenger; it is to encourage – or even push – companies to raise their aspirations and move to higher levels of competitive performance, even though this process may be inherently unpleasant and difficult. Government cannot create competitive industries; only companies can do that. Government plays a role that is inherently partial, that succeeds only when working in tandem with favorable underlying conditions in the diamond. Still, government's role of transmitting and amplifying the forces of the diamond is a powerful one. Government policies that succeed are those that create an environment in which compa-

> ## Competitive time for companies and political time for governments are fundamentally at odds.

nies can gain competitive advantage rather than those that involve government directly in the process, except in nations early in the development process. It is an indirect, rather than a direct, role.

Japan's government, at its best, understands this role better than anyone – including the point that nations pass through stages of competitive development and that government's appropriate role shifts as the economy progresses. By stimulating early demand for advanced products, confronting industries with the need to pioneer frontier technology through symbolic cooperative projects, establishing prizes that reward quality, and pursuing other policies that magnify the forces of the diamond, the Japanese government accelerates the pace of innovation. But like government officials anywhere, at their worst Japanese bureaucrats can make the same mistakes: attempting to manage industry structure, protecting the market too long, and yielding to political pressure to insulate inefficient retailers, farmers, distributors, and industrial companies from competition.

It is not hard to understand why so many governments make the same mistakes so often in pursuit of national competitiveness: competitive time for companies and political time for governments are fundamentally at odds. It often takes more than a decade for an industry to create competitive advantage; the process entails the long upgrading of human skills, investing in products and processes, building clusters, and penetrating foreign markets. In the case of the Japanese auto industry, for instance, companies made their first faltering steps toward exporting in the 1950s – yet did not achieve strong international positions until the 1970s.

But in politics, a decade is an eternity. Consequently, most governments favor policies that offer easily perceived short-term benefits, such as subsidies, protection, and arranged mergers – the very policies that retard innovation. Most of the policies that would make a real difference either are too slow and require too much patience for politicians or, even worse, carry with them the sting of short-term pain. Deregulating a protected industry, for example, will lead to bankruptcies sooner and to stronger, more competitive companies only later.

Policies that convey static, short-term cost advantages but that unconsciously undermine innovation and dynamism represent the most common and most profound error in government industrial policy. In a desire to help, it is all too easy for governments to adopt policies such as joint projects to avoid "wasteful" R&D that undermine dynamism and competition. Yet even a 10% cost saving through economies of scale is easily nullified through rapid product and process improvement and the pursuit of volume in global markets – something that such policies undermine.

There are some simple, basic principles that governments should embrace to play the proper supportive role for national competitiveness: encourage change, promote domestic rivalry, stimulate innovation. Some of the specific policy approaches to guide nations seeking to gain competitive advantage include the following:

Focus on specialized factor creation. Government has critical responsibilities for fundamentals like the primary and secondary education systems, basic national infrastructure, and research in areas of broad national concern such as health care. Yet these kinds of generalized efforts at factor creation rarely produce competitive advantage. Rather, the factors that translate into competitive advantage are advanced, specialized, and tied to specific industries or industry groups. Mechanisms such as specialized apprenticeship programs, research efforts in universities connected with an industry, trade association activities, and, most important, the private investments of companies ultimately create the factors that will yield competitive advantage.

Avoid intervening in factor and currency markets. By intervening in factor and currency markets, governments hope to create lower factor costs or a favorable exchange rate that will help companies compete more effectively in international markets. Evidence from around the world indicates that these policies – such as the Reagan administration's dollar devaluation – are often counterproductive. They work against the upgrading of industry and the search for more sustainable competitive advantage.

The contrasting case of Japan is particularly instructive, although both Germany and Switzerland have had similar experiences. Over the past 20 years, the Japanese have been rocked by the sudden Nixon currency devaluation shock, two oil shocks, and, most recently, the yen shock – all of which forced Japanese companies to upgrade their competitive advantages. The point is not that government should pursue policies that intentionally drive up factor costs or the exchange rate. Rather, when market forces create rising factor costs or a higher exchange rate, government should resist the temptation to push them back down.

Enforce strict product, safety, and environmental standards. Strict government regulations can promote competitive advantage by stimulating and upgrading domestic demand. Stringent standards for product performance, product safety, and environmental impact pressure companies to improve quality, upgrade technology, and provide features that respond to consumer and social demands. Easing standards, however tempting, is counterproductive.

When tough regulations anticipate standards that will spread internationally, they give a nation's companies a head start in developing products and services that will be valuable elsewhere. Sweden's strict standards for environmental protection have promoted competitive advantage in many industries. Atlas Copco, for example, produces quiet compressors that can be used in dense urban areas with minimal disruption to residents. Strict standards, however, must be combined with a rapid and streamlined regulatory process that does not absorb resources and cause delays.

Sharply limit direct cooperation among industry rivals. The most pervasive global policy fad in the competitiveness arena today is the call for more cooperative research and industry consortia. Operating on the belief that independent research by rivals is wasteful and duplicative, that collaborative efforts achieve economies of scale, and that individual com-

 Most Japanese companies participate in MITI research projects for defensive reasons.

panies are likely to underinvest in R&D because they cannot reap all the benefits, governments have embraced the idea of more direct cooperation. In the United States, antitrust laws have been modified to allow more cooperative R&D; in Europe, megaprojects such as ESPRIT, an information-technology project, bring together companies from several countries. Lurking behind much of this thinking is the fascination of Western governments with – and fundamental misunderstanding of – the countless cooperative research projects sponsored by the Ministry of International Trade and Industry (MITI), projects that appear to have contributed to Japan's competitive rise.

But a closer look at Japanese cooperative projects suggests a different story. Japanese companies participate in MITI projects to maintain good relations with MITI, to preserve their corporate images, and to hedge the risk that competitors will gain from the project – largely defensive reasons. Companies rarely contribute their best scientists and engineers to cooperative projects and usually spend much more on their own private research in the same field. Typically, the government makes only a modest financial contribution to the project.

The real value of Japanese cooperative research is to signal the importance of emerging technical areas and to stimulate proprietary company research. Cooperative projects prompt companies to explore new

Tax incentives for long-term capital gains encourage long-term investment.

fields and boost internal R&D spending because companies know that their domestic rivals are investigating them.

Under certain limited conditions, cooperative research can prove beneficial. Projects should be in areas of basic product and process research, not in subjects closely connected to a company's proprietary sources of advantage. They should constitute only a modest portion of a company's overall research program in any given field. Cooperative research should be only indirect, channeled through independent organizations to which most industry participants have access. Organizational structures, like university labs and centers of excellence, reduce management problems and minimize the risk to rivalry. Finally, the most useful cooperative projects often involve fields that touch a number of industries and that require substantial R&D investments.

Promote goals that lead to sustained investment. Government has a vital role in shaping the goals of investors, managers, and employees through policies in various areas. The manner in which capital markets are regulated, for example, shapes the incentives of investors and, in turn, the behavior of companies. Government should aim to encourage sustained investment in human skills, in innovation, and in

physical assets. Perhaps the single most powerful tool for raising the rate of sustained investment in industry is a tax incentive for long-term (five years or more) capital gains restricted to new investment in corporate equity. Long-term capital gains incentives should also be applied to pension funds and other currently untaxed investors, who now have few reasons not to engage in rapid trading.

Deregulate competition. Regulation of competition through such policies as maintaining a state monopoly, controlling entry into an industry, or fixing prices has two strong negative consequences: it stifles rivalry and innovation as companies become preoccupied with dealing with regulators and protecting what they already have; and it makes the industry a less dynamic and less desirable buyer or supplier. Deregulation and privatization on their own, however, will not succeed without vigorous domestic rivalry – and that requires, as a corollary, a strong and consistent antitrust policy.

Enforce strong domestic antitrust policies. A strong antitrust policy – especially for horizontal mergers, alliances, and collusive behavior – is fundamental to innovation. While it is fashionable today to call for mergers and alliances in the name of globalization and the creation of national champions, these often undermine the creation of competitive advantage. Real national competitiveness requires governments to disallow mergers, acquisitions, and alliances that involve industry leaders. Furthermore, the same standards for mergers and alliances should apply to both domestic and foreign companies. Finally, government policy should favor internal entry, both domestic and international, over acquisition. Companies should, however, be allowed to acquire small companies in related industries when the move promotes the transfer of skills that could ultimately create competitive advantage.

Reject managed trade. Managed trade represents a growing and dangerous tendency for dealing with the

Better than managed trade: pressure Japan to buy more manufactured imports.

fallout of national competitiveness. Orderly marketing agreements, voluntary restraint agreements, or other devices that set quantitative targets to divide up markets are dangerous, ineffective, and often enormously costly to consumers. Rather than promoting innovation in a nation's industries, managed trade guarantees a market for inefficient companies.

Government trade policy should pursue open market access in every foreign nation. To be effective, trade policy should not be a passive instrument; it cannot respond only to complaints or work only for those industries that can muster enough political clout; it should not require a long history of injury or serve only distressed industries. Trade policy should seek to open markets wherever a nation has competitive advantage and should actively address emerging industries and incipient problems.

Where government finds a trade barrier in another nation, it should concentrate its remedies on dismantling barriers, not on regulating imports or exports. In the case of Japan, for example, pressure to accelerate the already rapid growth of manufactured imports is a more effective approach than a shift to managed trade. Compensatory tariffs that punish companies for unfair trade practices are better than market quotas. Other increasingly important tools to open markets are restrictions that prevent companies in offending nations from investing in acquisitions or production facilities in the host country—thereby blocking the unfair country's companies from using their advantage to establish a new beachhead that is immune from sanctions.

Any of these remedies, however, can backfire. It is virtually impossible to craft remedies to unfair trade practices that avoid both reducing incentives for domestic companies to innovate and export and harming domestic buyers. The aim of remedies should be adjustments that allow the remedy to disappear.

The Company Agenda

Ultimately, only companies themselves can achieve and sustain competitive advantage. To do so, they must act on the fundamentals described above. In particular, they must recognize the central role of innovation—and the uncomfortable truth that innovation grows out of pressure and challenge. It takes leadership to create a dynamic, challenging environment. And it takes leadership to recognize the all-too-easy escape routes that appear to offer a path to competitive advantage, but are actually short-cuts to failure. For example, it is tempting to rely on cooperative research and development projects to lower the cost and risk of research. But they can divert company attention and resources from proprietary research efforts and will all but eliminate the prospects for real innovation.

Competitive advantage arises from leadership that harnesses and amplifies the forces in the diamond to promote innovation and upgrading. Here are just a few of the kinds of company policies that will support that effort:

Create pressures for innovation. A company should seek out pressure and challenge, not avoid them. Part of strategy is to take advantage of the home nation to create the impetus for innovation. To do that, companies can sell to the most sophisticated and demanding buyers and channels; seek out those buyers with the most difficult needs; establish norms that exceed the toughest regulatory hurdles or product standards; source from the most advanced suppliers; treat employees as permanent in order to stimulate upgrading of skills and productivity.

Seek out the most capable competitors as motivators. To motivate organizational change, capable competitors and respected rivals can be a common enemy. The best managers always run a little scared; they respect and study competitors. To stay dynamic, companies must make meeting challenge a part of the organization's norms. For example, lobbying against strict product standards signals the organization that company leadership has diminished aspirations. Companies that value stability, obedient customers, dependent suppliers, and sleepy competitors are inviting inertia and, ultimately, failure.

Establish early-warning systems. Early-warning signals translate into early-mover advantages. Companies can take actions that help them see the signals of change and act on them, thereby getting a jump on the competition. For example, they can find and serve those buyers with the most anticipatory needs; investigate all emerging new buyers or channels; find places whose regulations foreshadow emerging regulations elsewhere; bring some outsiders into the management team; maintain ongoing relationships with research centers and sources of talented people.

Improve the national diamond. Companies have a vital stake in making their home environment a better platform for international success. Part of a company's responsibility is to play an active role in forming clusters and to work with its home-nation buyers, suppliers, and channels to help them upgrade and extend their own competitive advantages. To upgrade home demand, for example, Japanese musical instrument manufacturers, led by Yamaha, Kawai, and Suzuki, have established music schools. Similarly, companies can stimulate and support local suppliers of important specialized inputs—including encouraging them to compete globally. The health and strength of the national cluster will only enhance the company's own rate of innovation and upgrading.

In nearly every successful competitive industry, leading companies also take explicit steps to create

How the Diamond Works:
The Italian Ceramic Tile Industry

In 1987, Italian companies were world leaders in the production and export of ceramic tiles, a $10 billion industry. Italian producers, concentrated in and around the small town of Sassuolo in the Emilia-Romagna region, accounted for about 30% of world production and almost 60% of world exports. The Italian trade surplus that year in ceramic tiles was about $1.4 billion.

The development of the Italian ceramic tile industry's competitive advantage illustrates how the diamond of national advantage works. Sassuolo's sustainable competitive advantage in ceramic tiles grew not from any static or historical advantage but from dynamism and change. Sophisticated and demanding local buyers, strong and unique distribution channels, and intense rivalry among local companies created constant pressure for innovation. Knowledge grew quickly from continuous experimentation and cumulative production experience. Private ownership of the companies and loyalty to the community spawned intense commitment to invest in the industry.

Tile producers benefited as well from a highly developed set of local machinery suppliers and other supporting industries, producing materials, services, and infrastructure. The presence of world-class, Italian-related industries also reinforced Italian strength in tiles. Finally, the geographic concentration of the entire cluster supercharged the whole process. Today foreign companies compete against an entire subculture. The organic nature of this system represents the most sustainable advantage of Sassuolo's ceramic tile companies.

The Origins of the Italian Industry

Tile production in Sassuolo grew out of the earthenware and crockery industry, whose history traces back to the thirteenth century. Immediately after World War II, there were only a handful of ceramic tile manufacturers in and around Sassuolo, all serving the local market exclusively.

Demand for ceramic tiles within Italy began to grow dramatically in the immediate postwar years, as the reconstruction of Italy triggered a boom in building materials of all kinds. Italian demand for ceramic tiles was particularly great due to the climate, local tastes, and building techniques.

Because Sassuolo was in a relatively prosperous part of Italy, there were many who could combine the modest amount of capital and necessary organizational skills to start a tile company. In 1955, there were 14 Sassuolo area tile companies; by 1962, there were 102.

The new tile companies benefited from a local pool of mechanically trained workers. The region around Sassuolo was home to Ferrari, Maserati, Lamborghini, and other technically sophisticated companies. As the tile industry began to grow and prosper, many engineers and skilled workers gravitated to the successful companies.

The Emerging Italian Tile Cluster

Initially, Italian tile producers were dependent on foreign sources of raw materials and production technology. In the 1950s, the principal raw materials used to make tiles were kaolin (white) clays. Since there were red- but no white-clay deposits near Sassuolo, Italian producers had to import the clays from the United Kingdom. Tile-making equipment was also imported in the 1950s and 1960s: kilns from Germany, America, and France; presses for forming tiles from Germany. Sassuolo tile makers had to import even simple glazing machines.

Over time, the Italian tile producers learned how to modify imported equipment to fit local circumstances: red versus white clays, natural gas versus heavy oil. As process technicians from tile companies left to start their own equipment companies, a local machinery industry arose in Sassuolo. By 1970, Italian companies had emerged as world-class producers of kilns and presses; the earlier situation had exactly reversed: they were exporting their red-clay equipment for foreigners to use with white clays.

The relationship between Italian tile and equipment manufacturers was a mutually supporting one, made even more so by close proximity. In the mid-1980s, there were some 200 Italian equipment manufacturers; more than 60% were located in the Sassuolo area. The equipment manufacturers competed fiercely for local business, and tile manufacturers benefited from better prices and more advanced equipment than their foreign rivals.

As the emerging tile cluster grew and concentrated in the Sassuolo region, a pool of skilled workers and technicians developed, including engineers, production specialists, maintenance workers, service technicians, and design personnel. The industry's geographic concentration encouraged other supporting companies to form, offering molds, packaging materials, glazes, and transportation services. An array of small, specialized consulting companies emerged to give advice to tile producers on plant design, logistics, and commercial, advertising, and fiscal matters.

With its membership concentrated in the Sassuolo area, Assopiastrelle, the ceramic tile industry association, began offering services in areas of common interest: bulk purchasing, foreign-market research, and consulting on fiscal and legal matters. The growing tile cluster stimulated the formation of a new, specialized factor-creating institution: in 1976, a consortium of the University of Bologna, regional agencies, and the ceramic industry association founded the Centro Ceramico di Bologna, which conducted process research and product analysis.

Sophisticated Home Demand

By the mid-1960s, per-capita tile consumption in Italy was considerably higher than in the rest of the world. The Italian market was also the world's most sophisticated. Italian customers, who were generally the first to adopt new designs and features, and Italian producers, who constantly innovated to improve manufacturing methods and create new designs, progressed in a mutually reinforcing process.

The uniquely sophisticated character of domestic demand also extended to retail outlets. In the 1960s, specialized tile showrooms began opening in Italy. By 1985, there were roughly 7,600 specialized showrooms handling approximately 80% of domestic sales, far more than in other nations. In 1976, the Italian company Piemme introduced tiles by famous designers to gain distribution outlets and to build brand name awareness among consumers. This innovation drew on another related industry, design services, in which Italy was world leader, with over $10 billion in exports.

Sassuolo Rivalry

The sheer number of tile companies in the Sassuolo area created intense rivalry. News of product and process innovations spread rapidly, and companies seeking technological, design, and distribution leadership had to improve constantly.

Proximity added a personal note to the intense rivalry. All of the producers were privately held, most were family run. The owners all lived in the same area, knew each other, and were the leading citizens of the same towns.

Pressures to Upgrade

In the early 1970s, faced with intense domestic rivalry, pressure from retail customers, and the shock of the 1973 energy crisis, Italian tile companies struggled to reduce gas and labor costs. These efforts led to a technological breakthrough, the rapid single-firing process, in which the hardening process, material transformation, and glaze-fixing all occurred in one pass through the kiln. A process that took 225 employees using the double-firing method needed only 90 employees using single-firing roller kilns. Cycle time dropped from 16 to 20 hours to only 50 to 55 minutes.

The new, smaller, and lighter equipment was also easier to export. By the early 1980s, exports from Italian equipment manufacturers exceeded domestic sales; in 1988, exports represented almost 80% of total sales.

Working together, tile manufacturers and equipment manufacturers made the next important breakthrough during the mid- and late 1970s: the development of materials-handling equipment that transformed tile manufacture from a batch process to a continuous process. The innovation reduced high labor costs—which had been a substantial selective factor disadvantage facing Italian tile manufacturers.

The common perception is that Italian labor costs were lower during this period than those in the United States and Germany. In those two countries, however, different jobs had widely different wages. In Italy, wages for different skill categories were compressed, and work rules constrained manufacturers from using overtime or multiple shifts. The restriction proved costly: once cool, kilns are expensive to reheat and are best run continuously. Because of this factor disadvantage, the Italian companies were the first to develop continuous, automated production.

Internationalization

By 1970, Italian domestic demand had matured. The stagnant Italian market led companies to step up their efforts to pursue foreign markets. The presence of related and supporting Italian industries helped in the export drive. Individual tile manufacturers began advertising in Italian and foreign home-design and architectural magazines, publications with wide global circulation among architects, designers, and consumers. This heightened awareness reinforced the quality image of Italian tiles. Tile makers were also able to capitalize on Italy's leading world export positions in related industries like marble, building stone, sinks, washbasins, furniture, lamps, and home appliances.

Assopiastrelle, the industry association, established trade-promotion offices in the United States in 1980, in Germany in 1984, and in France in 1987. It organized elaborate trade shows in cities ranging from Bologna to Miami and ran sophisticated advertising. Between 1980 and 1987, the association spent roughly $8 million to promote Italian tiles in the United States.

—Michael J. Enright and Paolo Tenti

Michael J. Enright, a doctoral student in business economics at the Harvard Business School, performed numerous research and supervisory tasks for The Competitive Advantage of Nations. *Paolo Tenti was responsible for the Italian part of research undertaken for the book. He is a consultant in strategy and finance for Monitor Company and Analysis F.A.—Milan.*

specialized factors like human resources, scientific knowledge, or infrastructure. In industries like wool cloth, ceramic tiles, and lighting equipment, Italian industry associations invest in market information, process technology, and common infrastructure. Companies can also speed innovation by putting their headquarters and other key operations where there are concentrations of sophisticated buyers, important suppliers, or specialized factor-creating mechanisms, such as universities or laboratories.

Welcome domestic rivalry. To compete globally, a company needs capable domestic rivals and vigorous domestic rivalry. Especially in the United States and Europe today, managers are wont to complain about excessive competition and to argue for mergers and acquisitions that will produce hoped-for economies of scale and critical mass. The complaint is only natural—but the argument is plain wrong. Vigorous domestic rivalry creates sustainable competitive advantage. Moreover, it is better to grow internationally than to dominate the domestic market. If a company wants an acquisition, a foreign one that can speed globalization and supplement home-based advantages or offset home-based disadvantages is usually far better than merging with leading domestic competitors.

> ## Innovating to overcome local disadvantages is better than outsourcing; developing domestic supplies is better than relying on foreign ones.

Globalize to tap selective advantages in other nations. In search of "global" strategies, many companies today abandon their home diamond. To be sure, adopting a global perspective is important to creating competitive advantage. But relying on foreign activities that supplant domestic capabilities is always a second-best solution. Innovating to offset local factor disadvantages is better than outsourcing; developing domestic suppliers and buyers is better than relying solely on foreign ones. Unless the critical underpinnings of competitiveness are present at home, companies will not sustain competitive advantage in the long run. The aim should be to upgrade home-base capabilities so that foreign activities are selective and supplemental only to over-all competitive advantage.

The correct approach to globalization is to tap selectively into sources of advantage in other nations' diamonds. For example, identifying sophisticated buyers in other countries helps companies understand different needs and creates pressures that will stimulate a faster rate of innovation. No matter how favorable the home diamond, moreover, important research is going on in other nations. To take advantage of foreign research, companies must station high-quality people in overseas bases and mount a credible level of scientific effort. To get anything back from foreign research ventures, companies must also allow access to their own ideas—recognizing that competitive advantage comes from continuous improvement, not from protecting today's secrets.

Use alliances only selectively. Alliances with foreign companies have become another managerial fad and cure-all: they represent a tempting solution to the problem of a company wanting the advantages of foreign enterprises or hedging against risk, without giving up independence. In reality, however, while alliances can achieve selective benefits, they always exact significant costs: they involve coordinating two separate operations, reconciling goals with an independent entity, creating a competitor, and giving up profits. These costs ultimately make most alliances short-term transitional devices, rather than stable, long-term relationships.

Author's note: Michael J. Enright, who served as project coordinator for this study, has contributed valuable suggestions.

Most important, alliances as a broad-based strategy will only ensure a company's mediocrity, not its international leadership. No company can rely on another outside, independent company for skills and assets that are central to its competitive advantage. Alliances are best used as a selective tool, employed on a temporary basis or involving noncore activities.

Locate the home base to support competitive advantage. Among the most important decisions for multinational companies is the nation in which to locate the home base for each distinct business. A company can have different home bases for distinct businesses or segments. Ultimately, competitive advantage is created at home: it is where strategy is set, the core product and process technology is created, and a critical mass of production takes place. The circumstances in the home nation must support innovation; otherwise the company has no choice but to move its home base to a country that stimulates innovation and that provides the best environment for global competitiveness. There are no half-measures: the management team must move as well.

The Role of Leadership

Too many companies and top managers misperceive the nature of competition and the task before them by focusing on improving financial performance, soliciting government assistance, seeking stability, and reducing risk through alliances and mergers.

> Using alliances as a strategy will only ensure a company's mediocrity, not its international leadership.

Today's competitive realities demand leadership. Leaders believe in change; they energize their organizations to innovate continuously; they recognize the importance of their home country as integral to their competitive success and work to upgrade it. Most important, leaders recognize the need for pressure and challenge. Because they are willing to encourage appropriate – and painful – government policies and regulations, they often earn the title "statesmen," although few see themselves that way. They are prepared to sacrifice the easy life for difficulty and, ultimately, sustained competitive advantage. That must be the goal, for both nations and companies: not just surviving, but achieving international competitiveness.

And not just once, but continuously.

Reprint 90211

READ THE FINE PRINT

HOW CAN *HARVARD BUSINESS REVIEW* ARTICLES WORK FOR YOU?

For years, we've printed a microscopically small notice on the editorial credits page of the *Harvard Business Review* alerting our readers to the availability of *HBR* articles.

Now we invite you to take a closer look at how you can put this hard-working business tool to work for you.

IN THE CORPORATE CLASSROOM

There's no more effective, or cost-effective, way to supplement your corporate training programs than in-depth, incisive *HBR* articles.

At just $3.50 a copy—even less for quantity orders—it's no wonder hundreds of companies use *HBR* articles for management training.

IN-BOX INNOVATION

Where do your company's movers and shakers get their big ideas? Many find inspiration in the pages of *HBR*. They then share the wealth by distributing *HBR* articles to colleagues.

IN MARKETING AND SALES SUPPORT

HBR articles are a substantive leave-behind to your sales calls. They add credibility to your direct mail campaigns. And demonstrate that your company is on the leading edge of business thinking.

CREATE CUSTOM ARTICLES

If you want even greater impact, personalize *HBR* articles with your company's name or logo. And put your name in front of your customers.

DISCOVER MORE REASONS IN THE *HBR CATALOG.*

In all, the *Harvard Business Review Catalog* lists articles on over 500 different subjects. Plus, you'll find collections, books, and videos on subjects you need to know. The catalog is yours for just $10.00. Order today. And start putting *HBR* articles to work for you.